FOR ORGANS, PIANOS & ELECTRONIC KEYBOARDS

**33**

# RAGTIME
## CLASSICS

ISBN 978-1-4950-6500-2

# HAL•LEONARD®
7777 W. BLUEMOUND RD. P.O. BOX 13819 MILWAUKEE, WI 53213

In Australia Contact:
**Hal Leonard Australia Pty. Ltd.**
4 Lentara Court
Cheltenham, Victoria, 3192 Australia
Email: ausadmin@halleonard.com.au

Visit Hal Leonard Online at
**www.halleonard.com**

# A Black Smoke

Registration 8
Rhythm: Fox Trot

By Charles L. Johnson

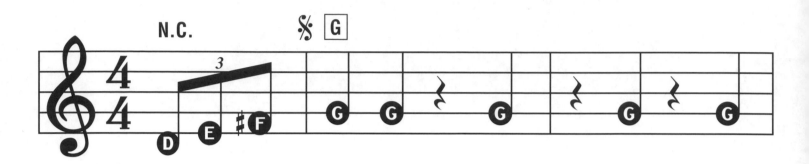

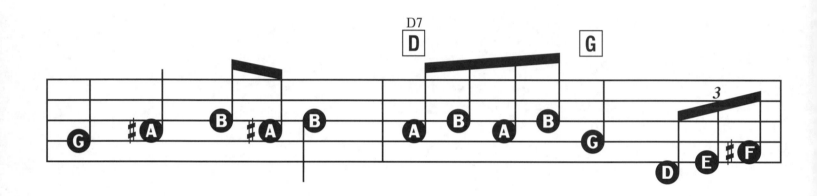

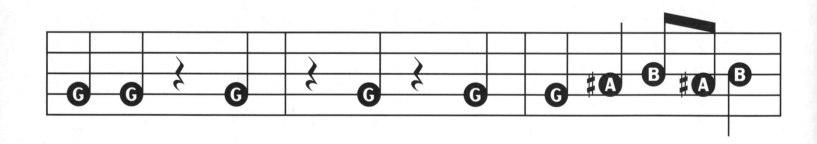

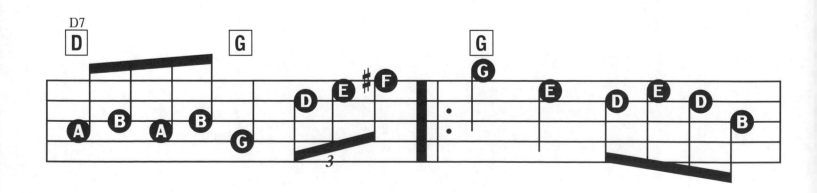

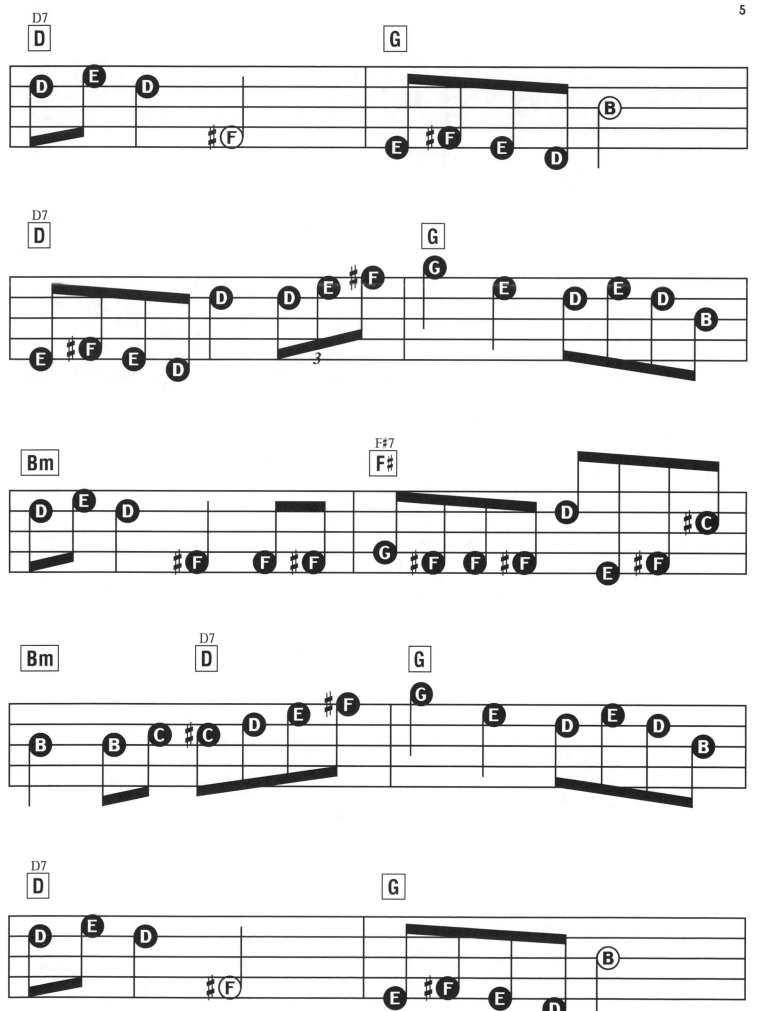

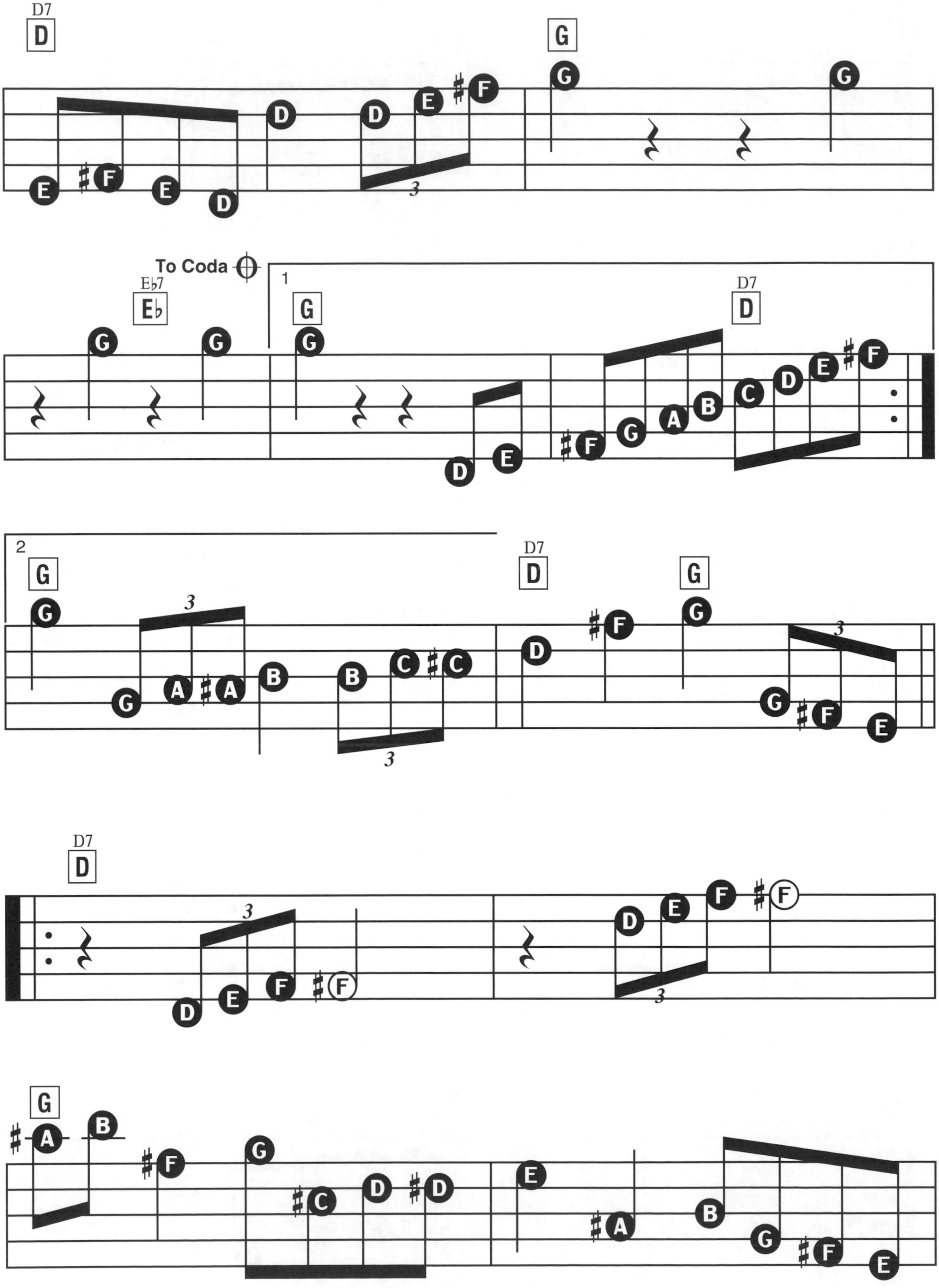
D7
D
G
To Coda
E♭7
E♭
1
G
D7
D
2
G
D7
D
G
D7
D
G

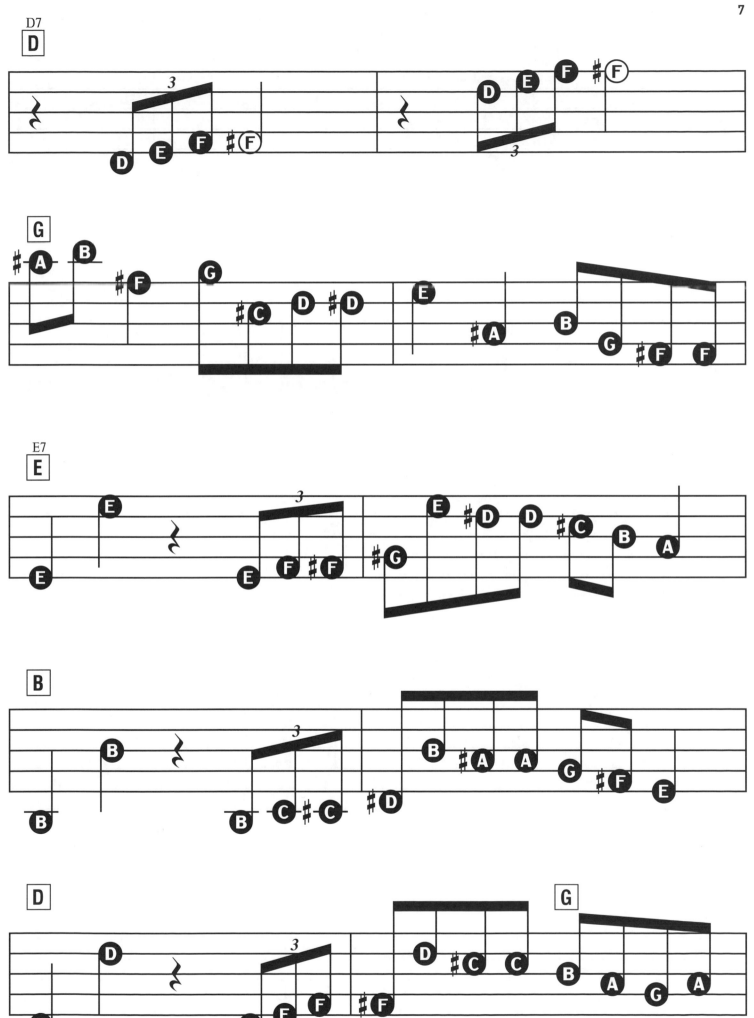

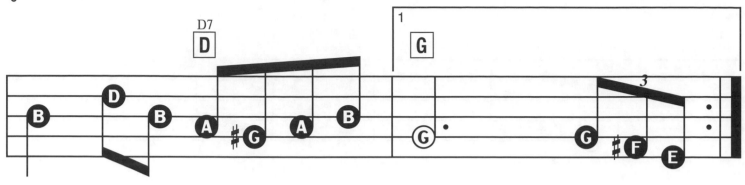

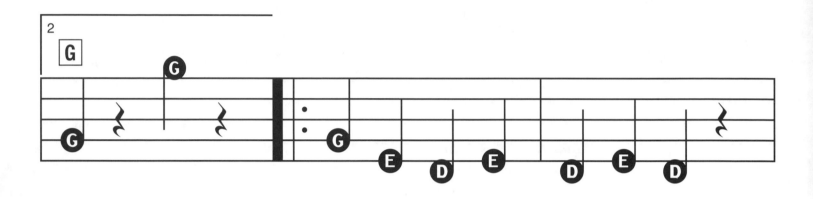

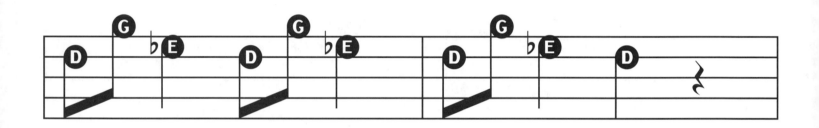

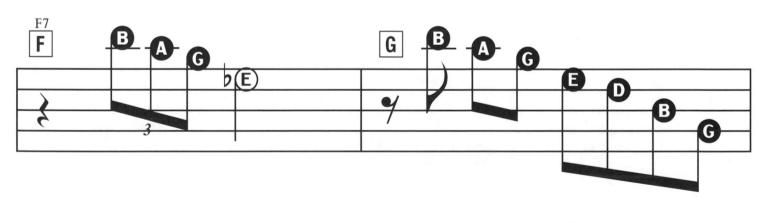

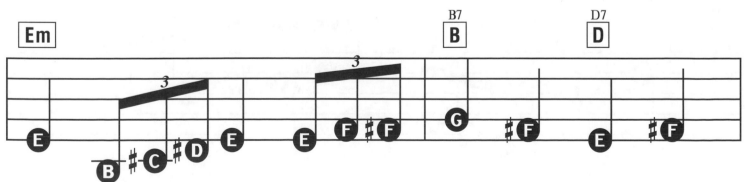

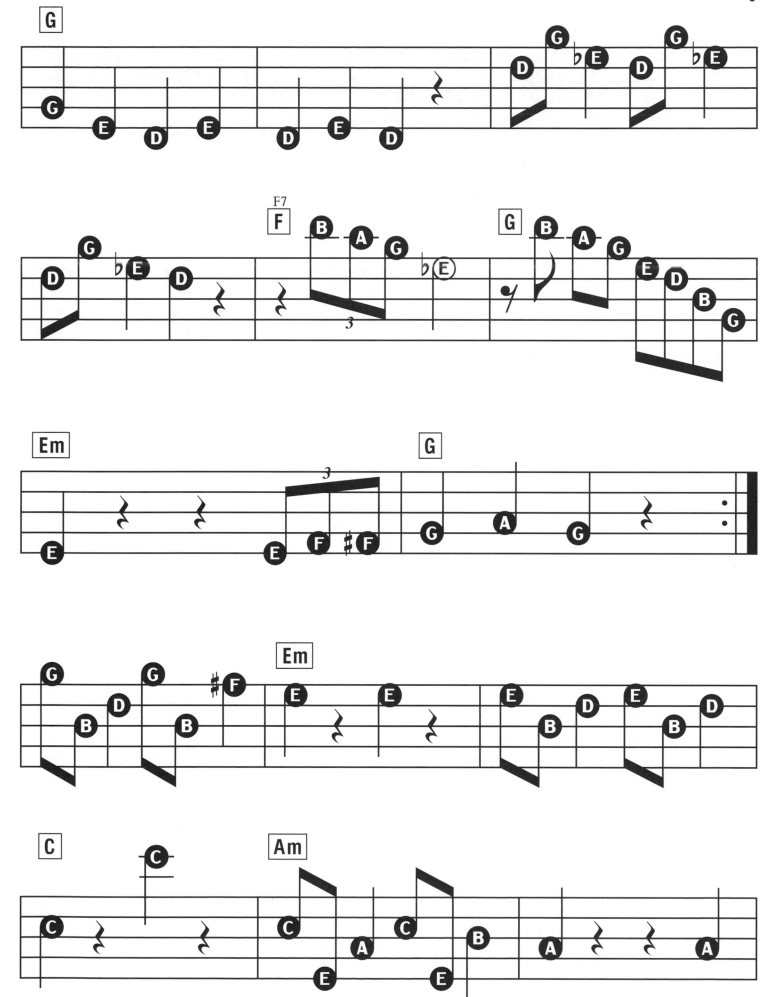

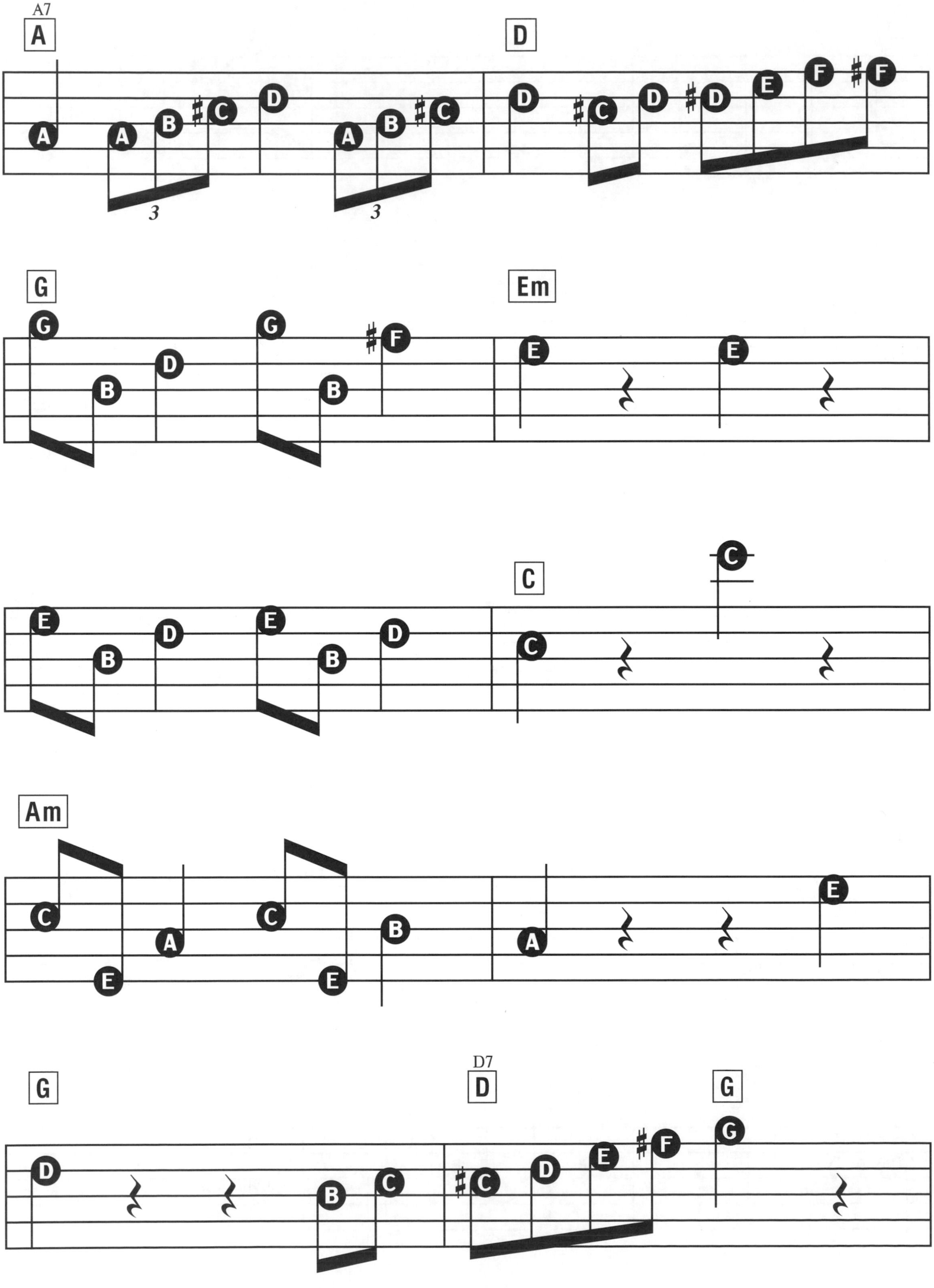
A7
A
D
G
Em
C
Am
G
D7
D
G

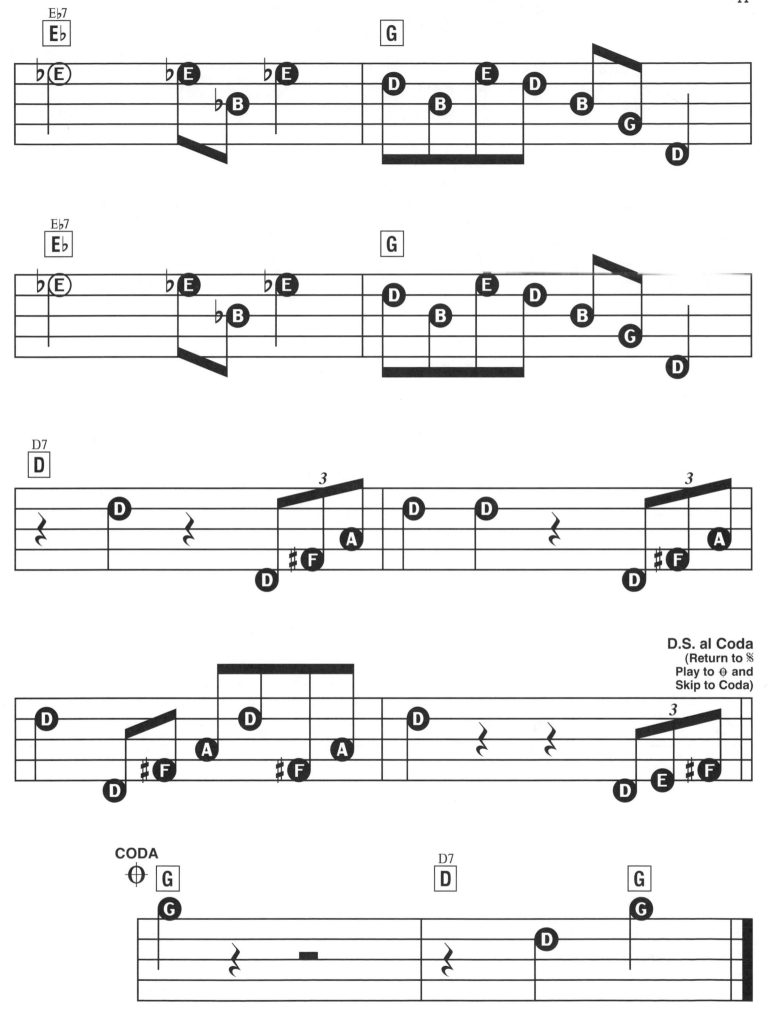

# Champagne Rag

Registration 8
Rhythm: Fox Trot

By Joseph Lamb

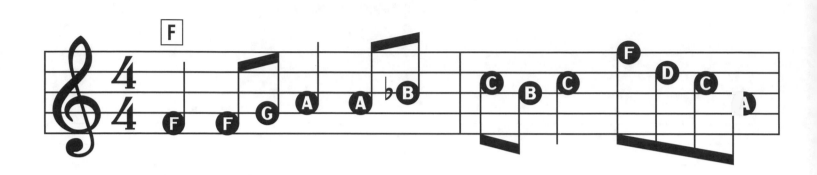

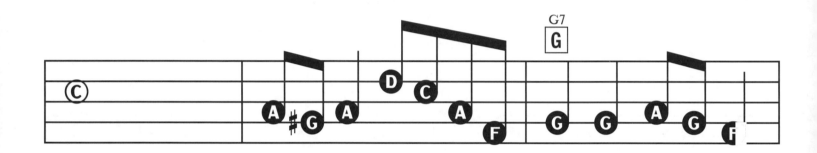

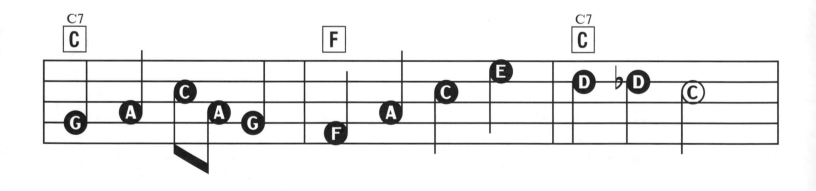

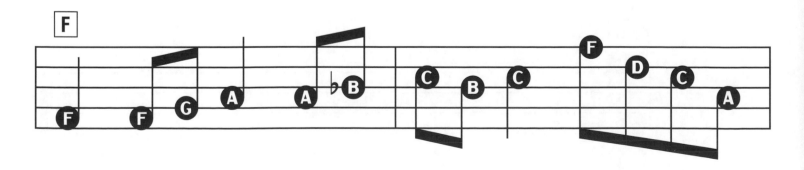

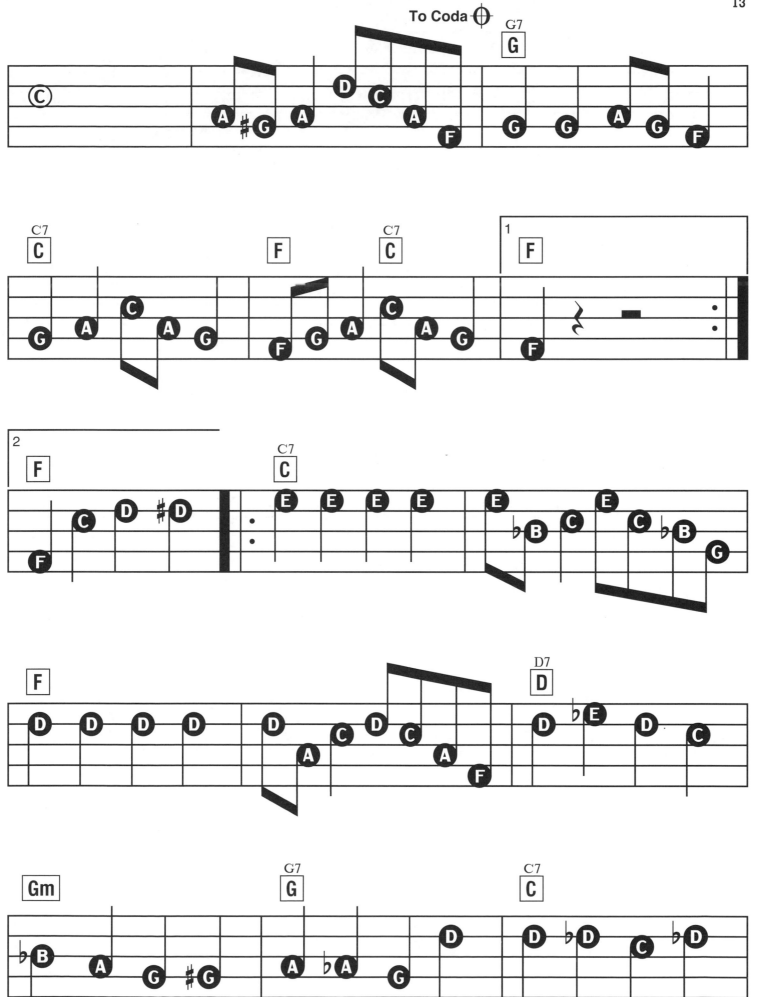

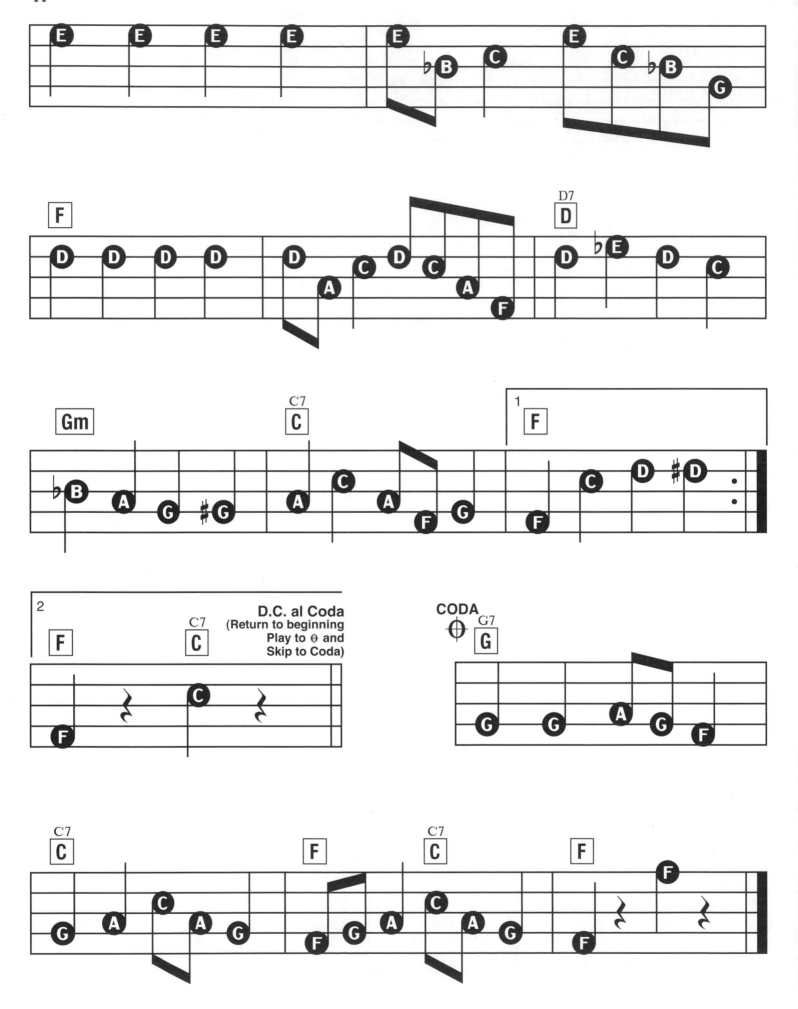

# Dimples

Registration 8
Rhythm: Fox Trot

By L.E. Colburn

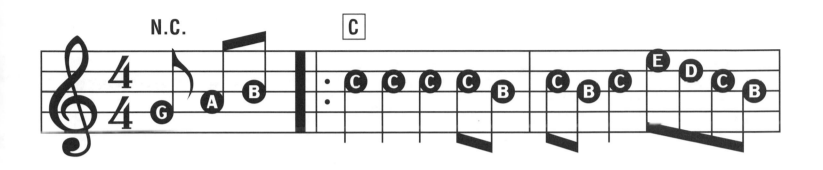

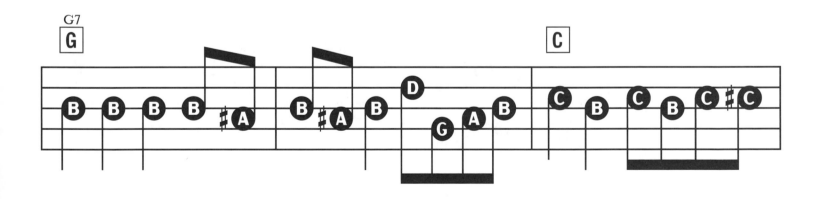

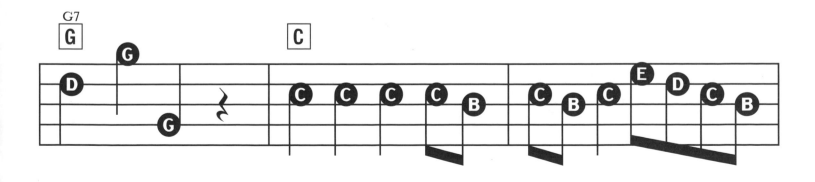

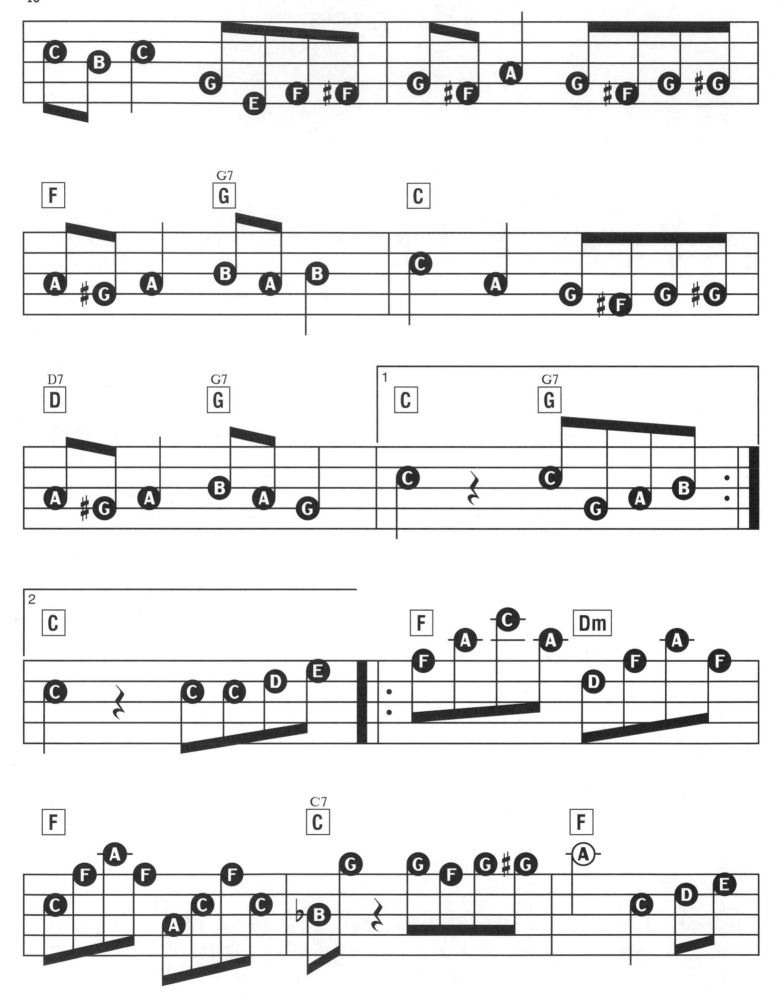

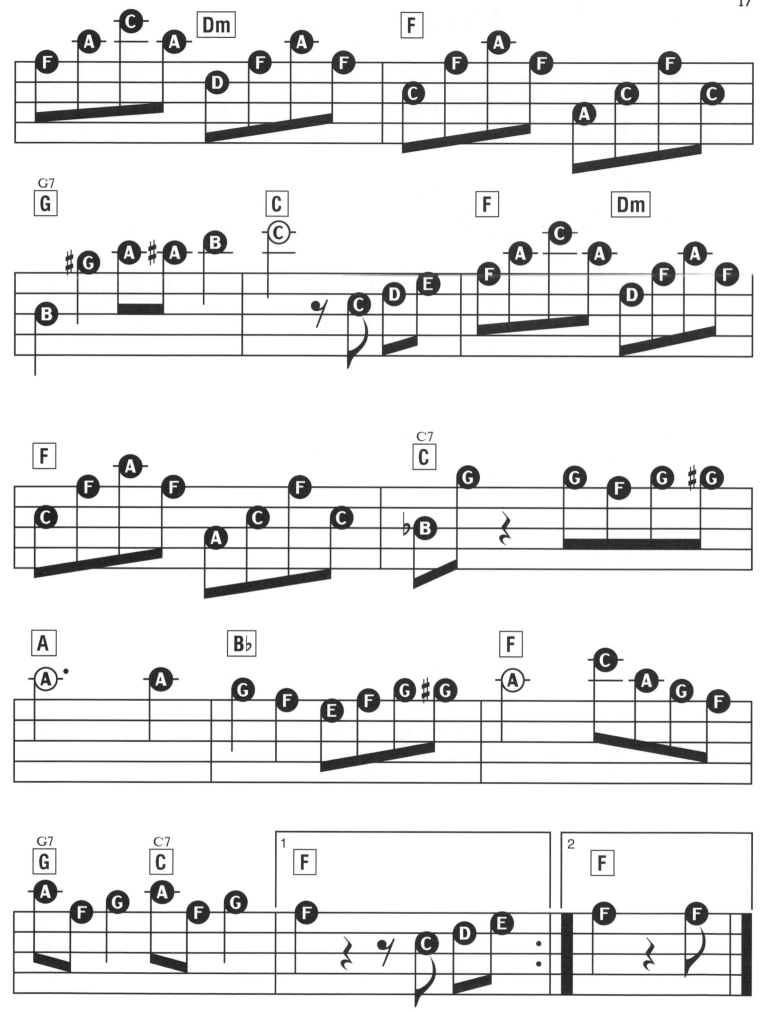

# Dill Pickles

Registration 8
Rhythm: Fox Trot

By Charles Johnson

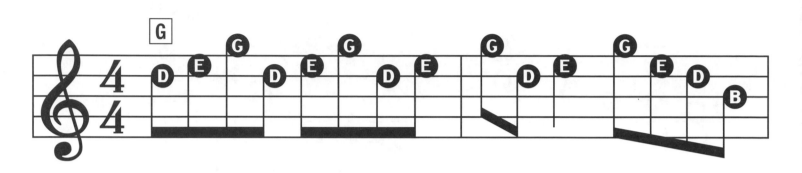

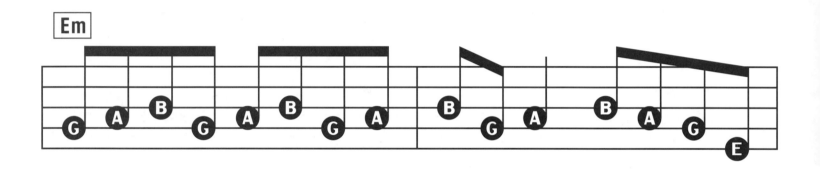

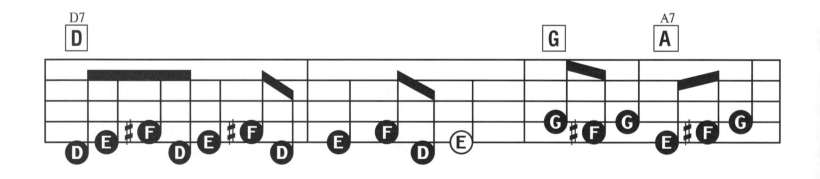

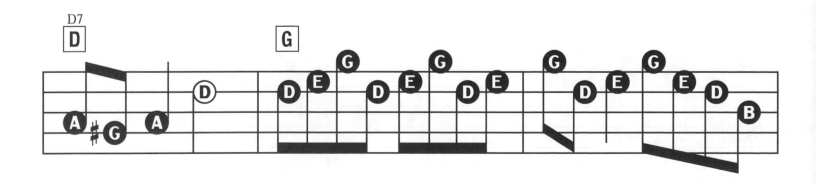

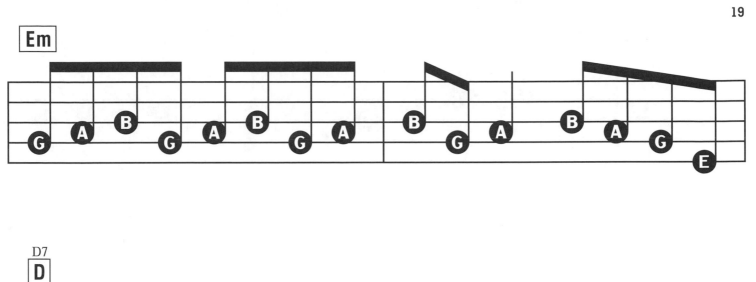

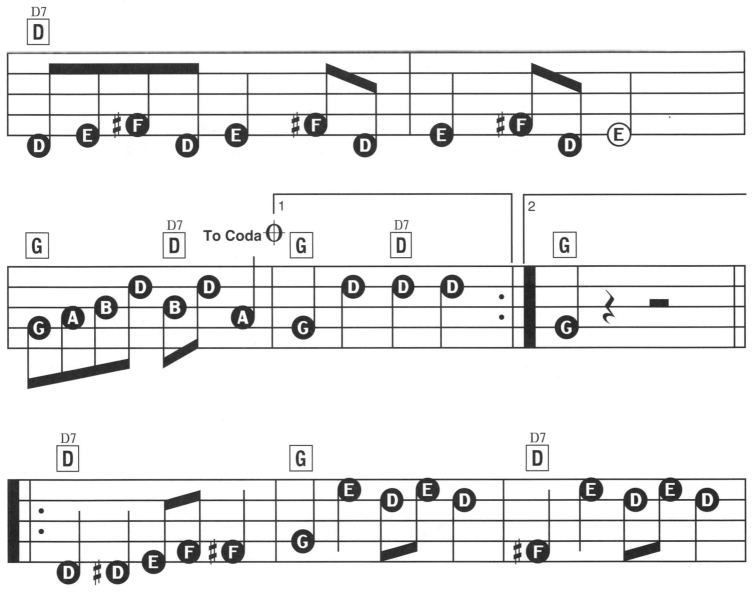

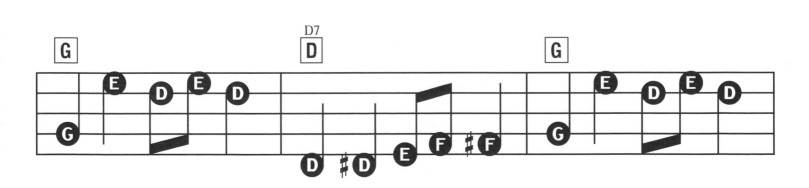

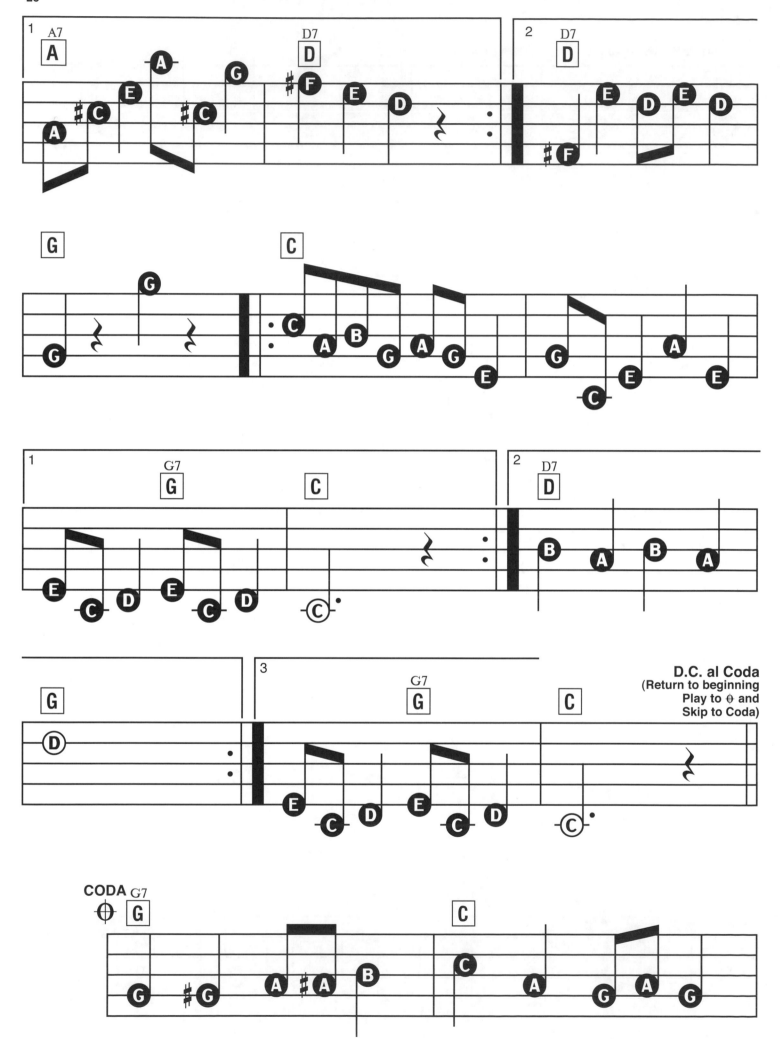

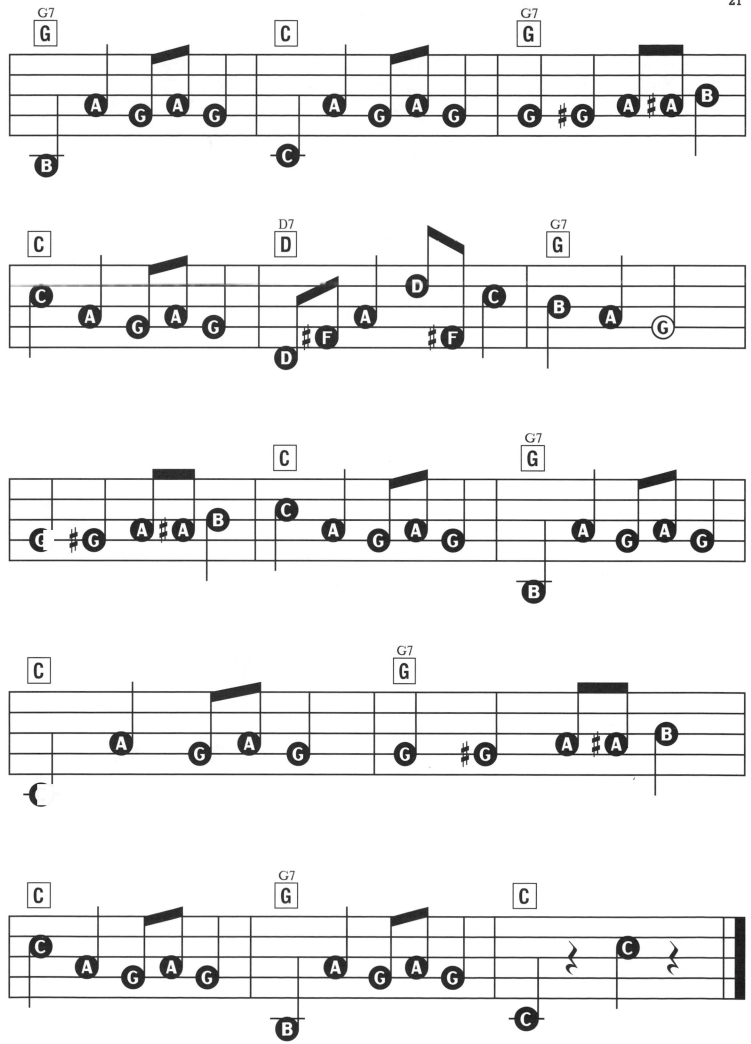

# The Entertainer

Registration 8
Rhythm: March or Polka

By Scott Joplin

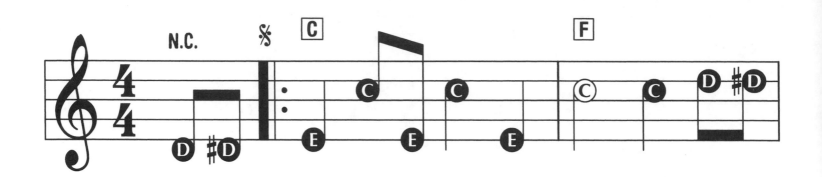

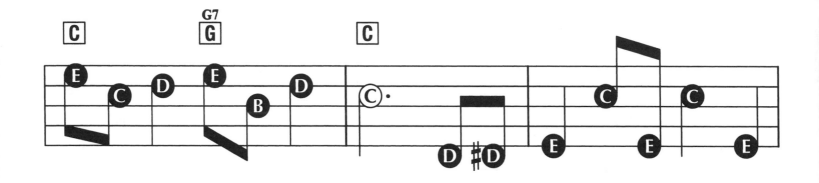

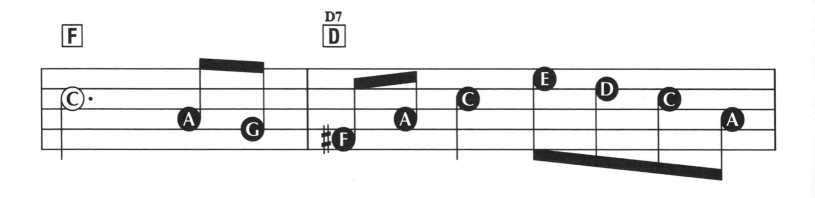

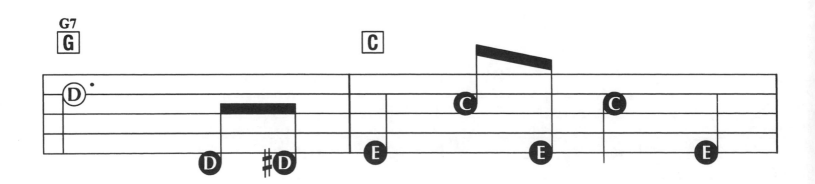

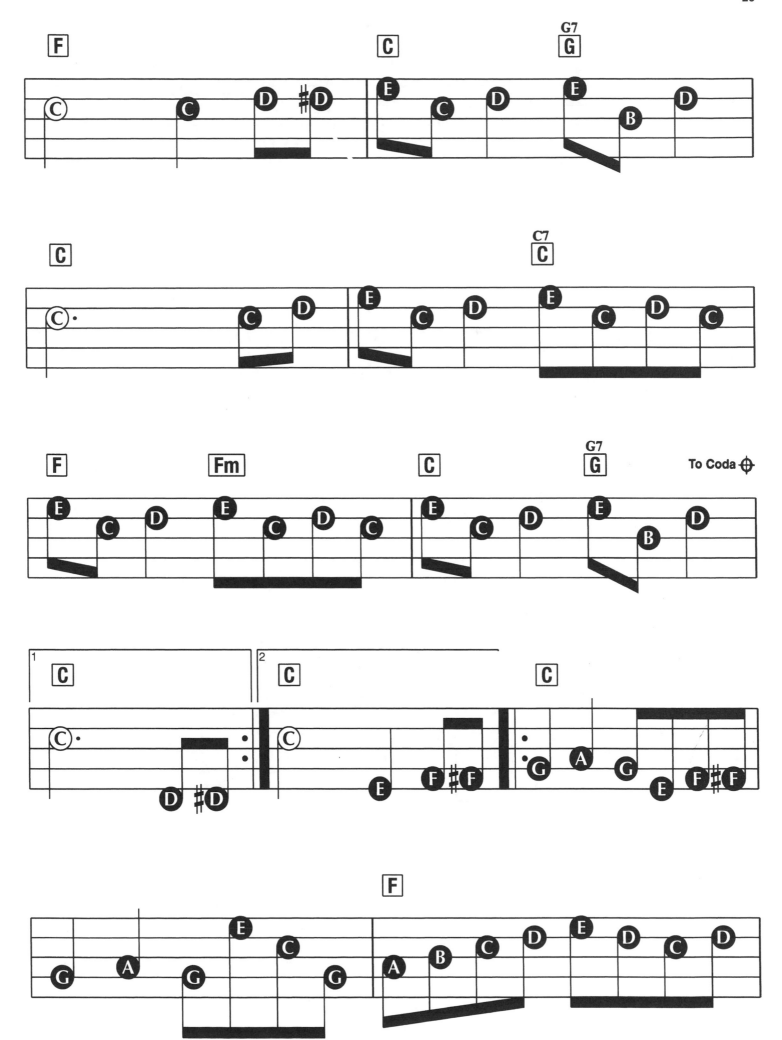

# Felicity Rag

Registration 8
Rhythm: Fox Trot

By Scott Joplin
and Scott Hayden

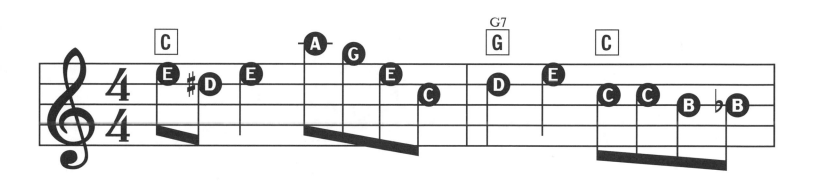

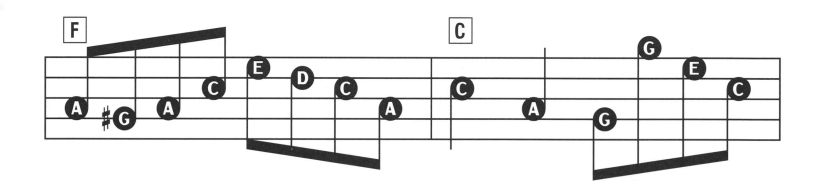

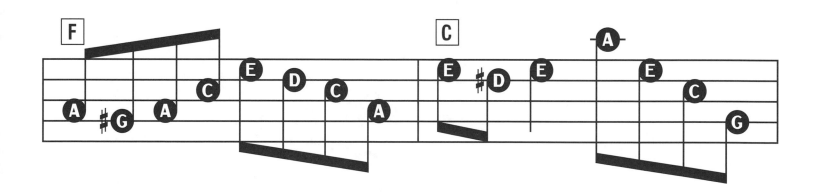

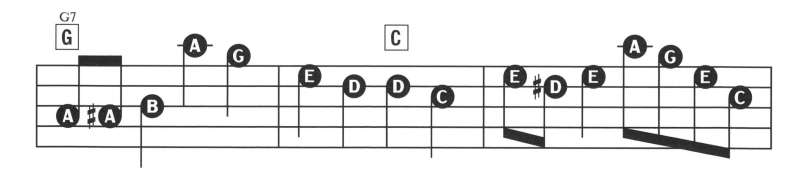

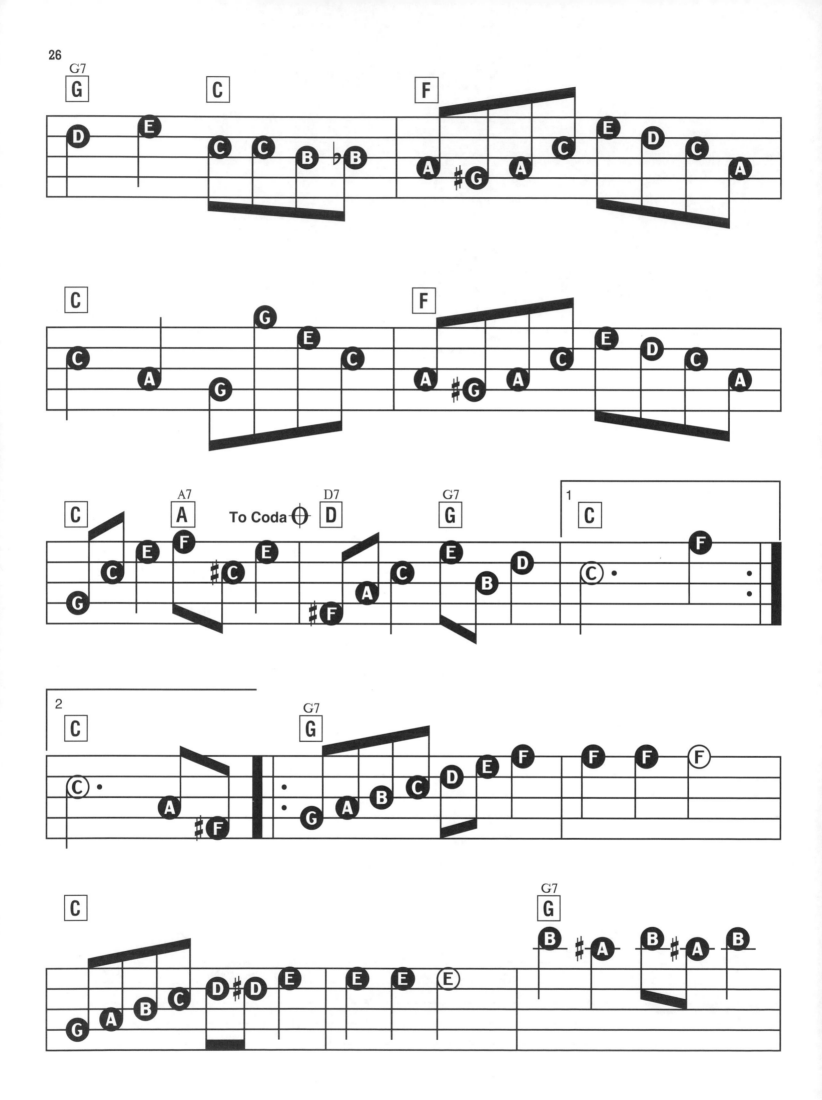

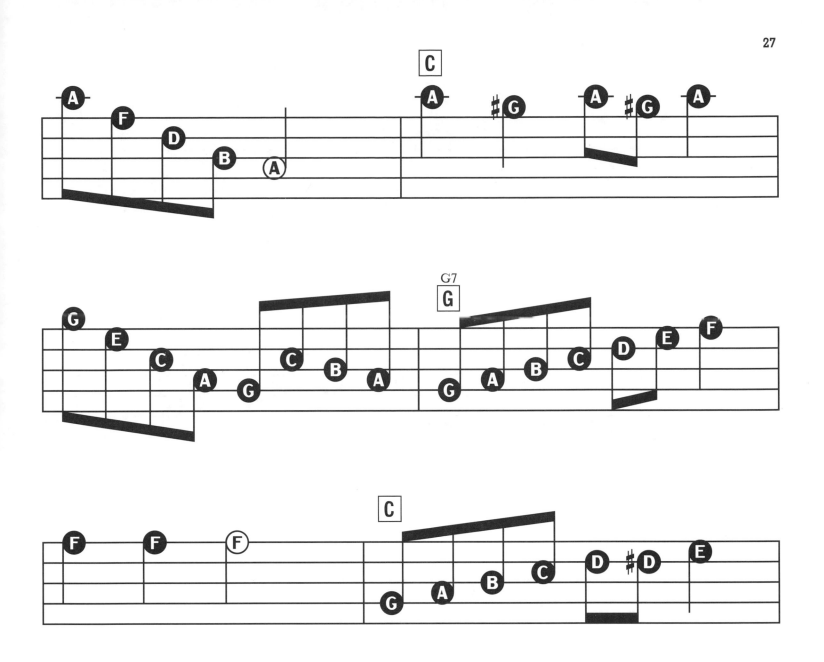

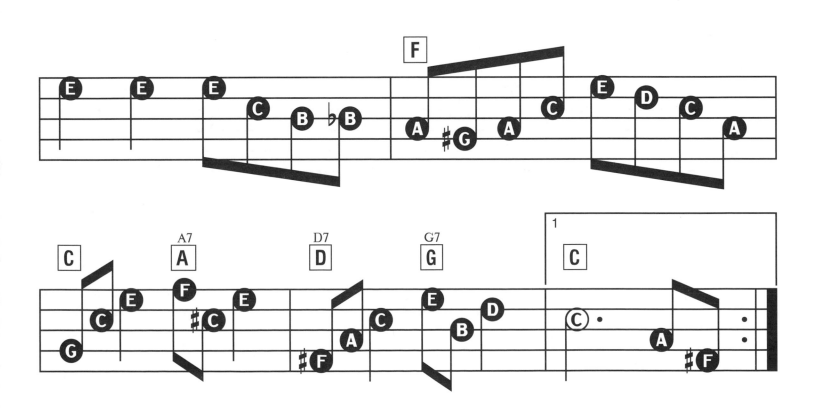

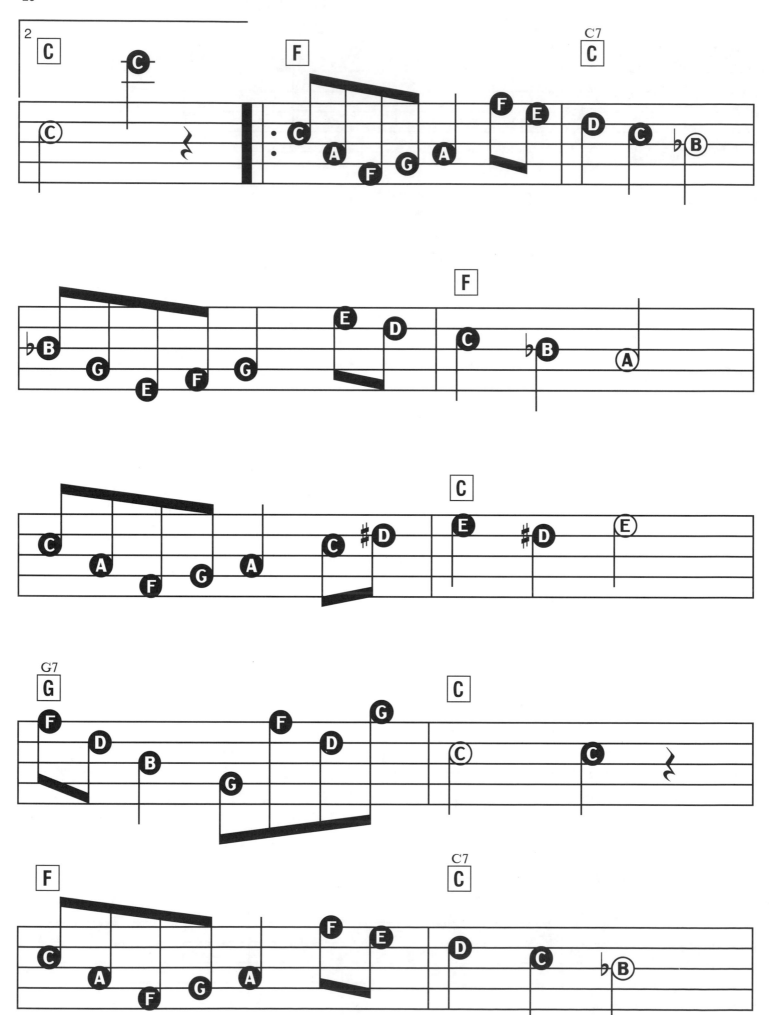

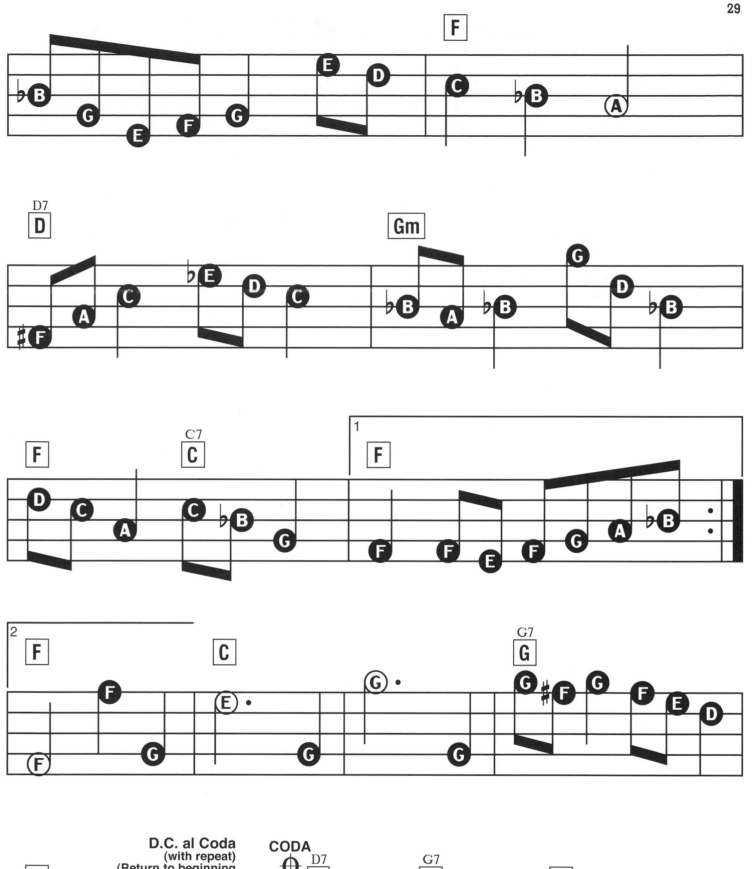

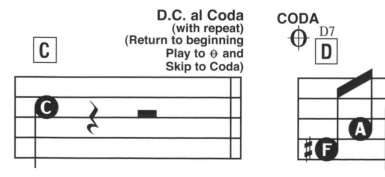

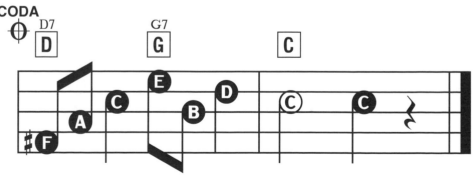

# Maple Leaf Rag

Registration 8
Rhythm: March or Polka

By Scott Joplin

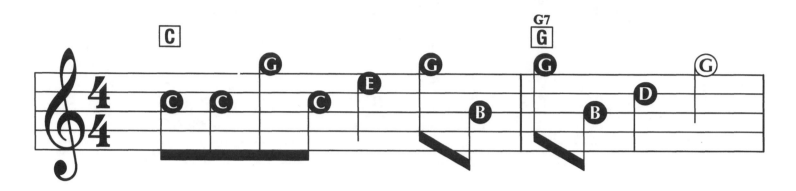

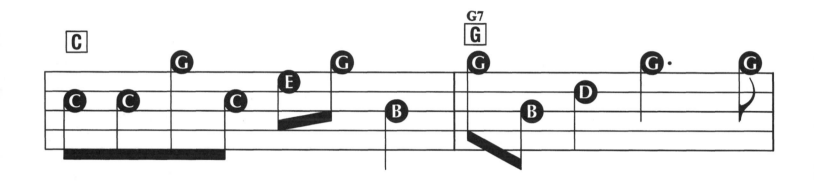

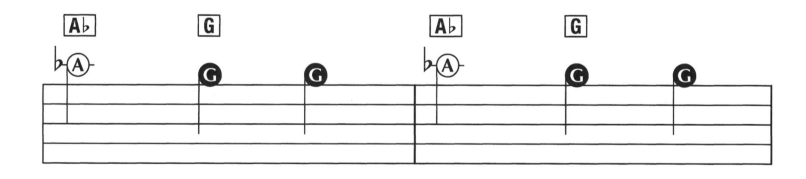

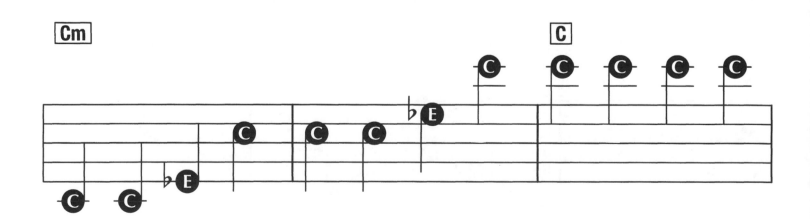

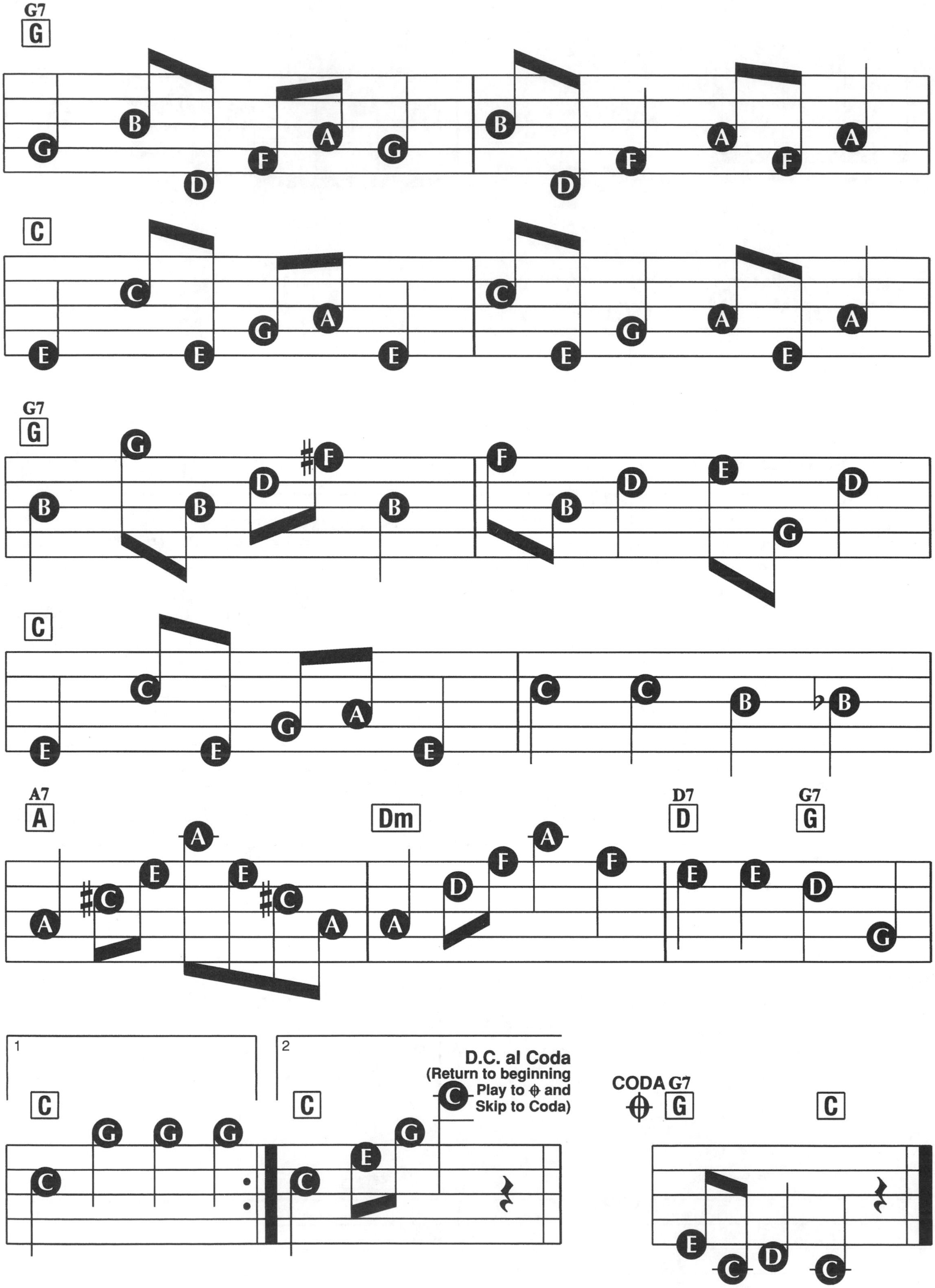
G7
G
C
G7
G
C
A7
A
Dm
D7
D
G7
G
1
C
2
C
D.C. al Coda
(Return to beginning
Play to ⊕ and
Skip to Coda)
CODA G7
G
C

# Peaches and Cream

Registration 8
Rhythm: Fox Trot

By Percy Wenrich

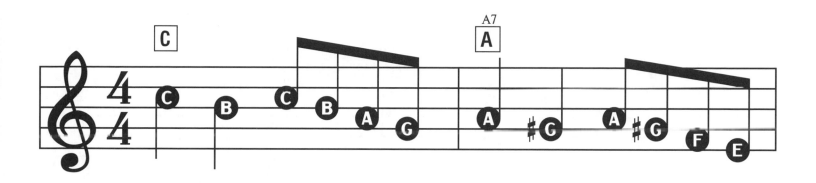

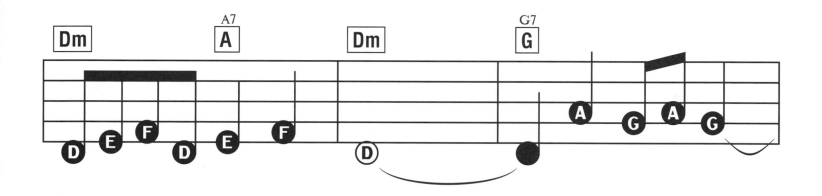

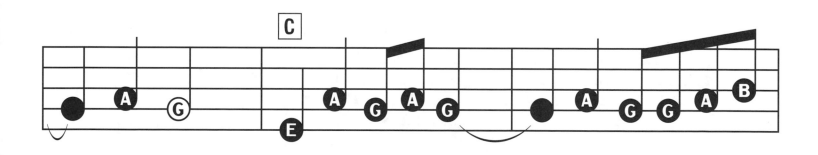

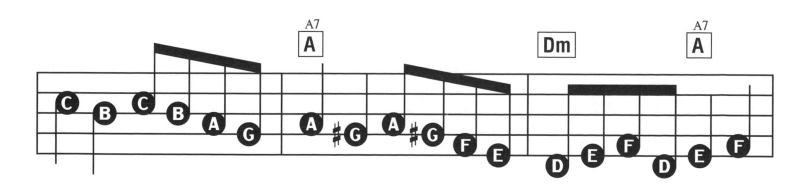

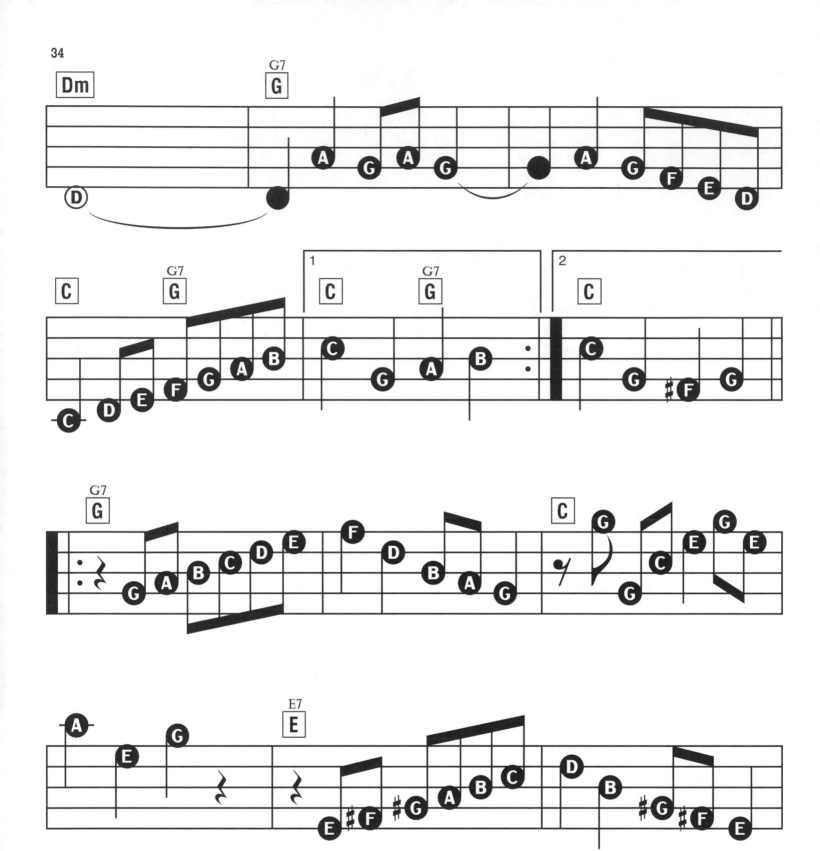

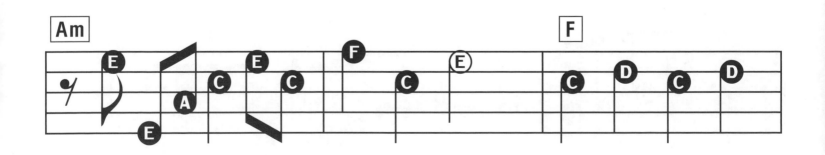

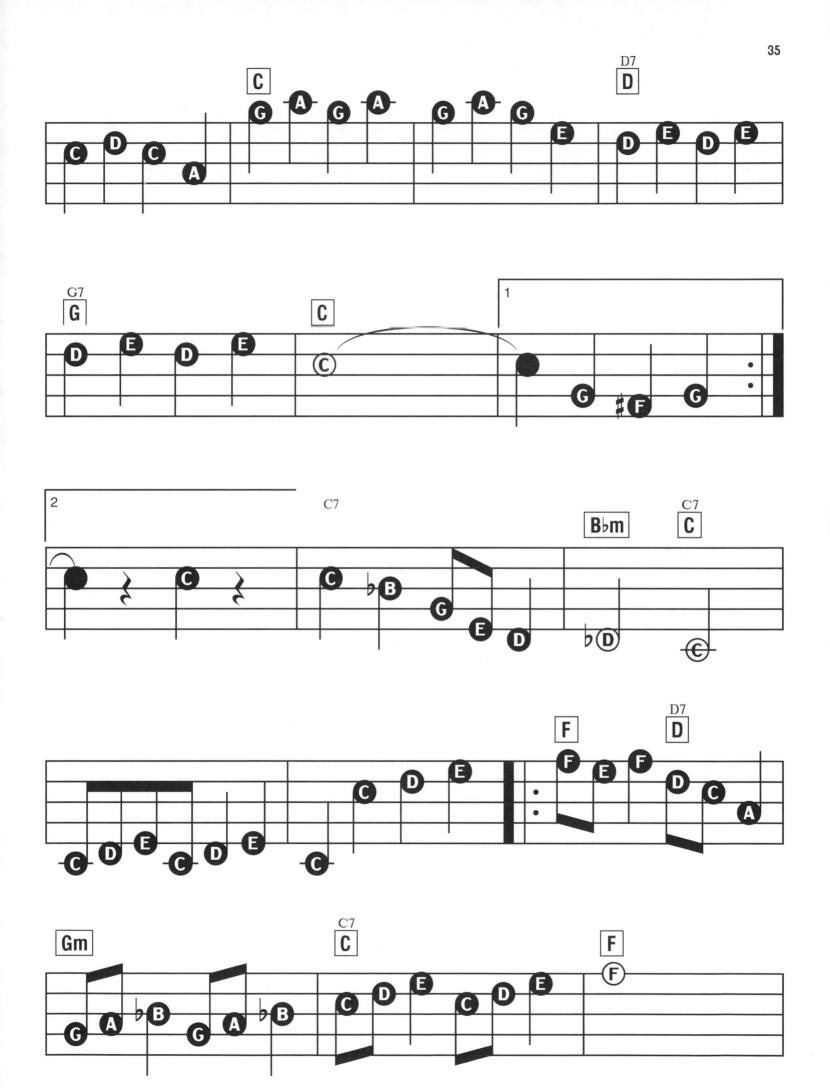

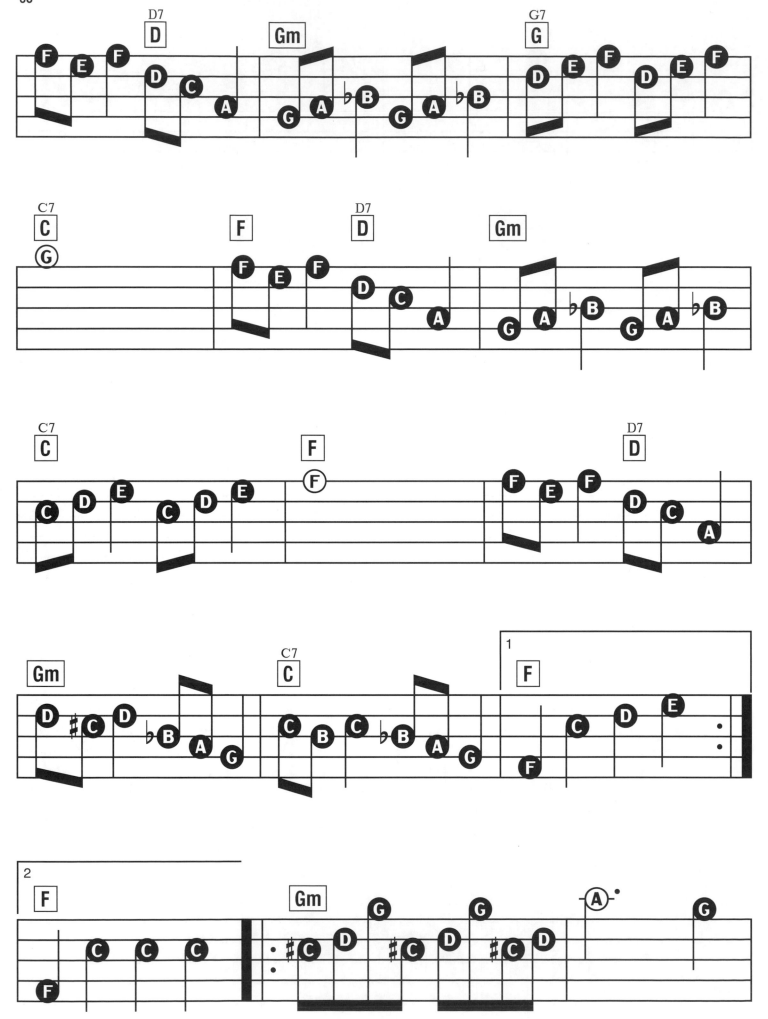

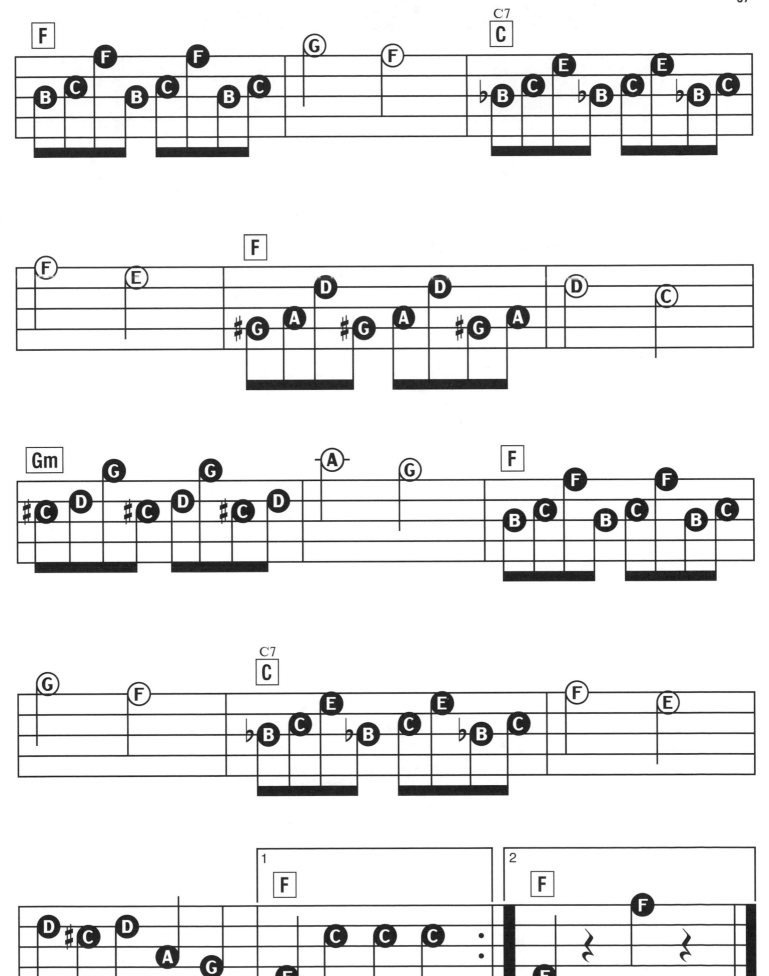

# Pride of Bucktown

Registration 8
Rhythm: Fox Trot

By Robert S. Roberts

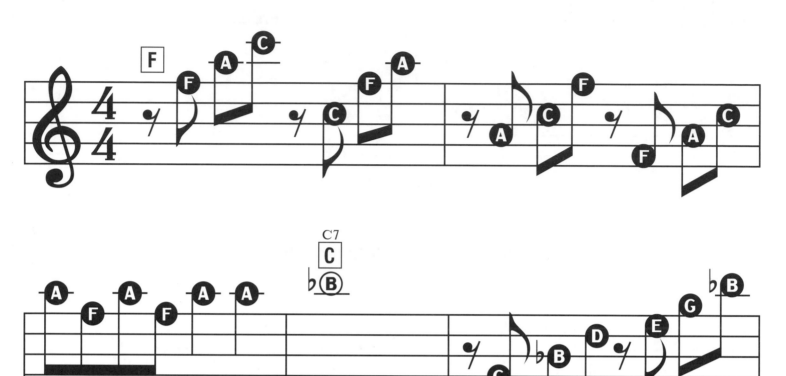

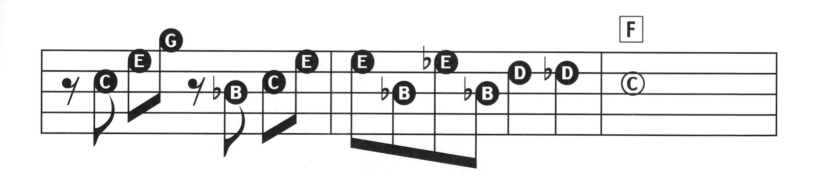

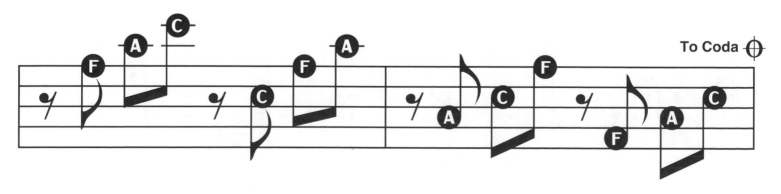

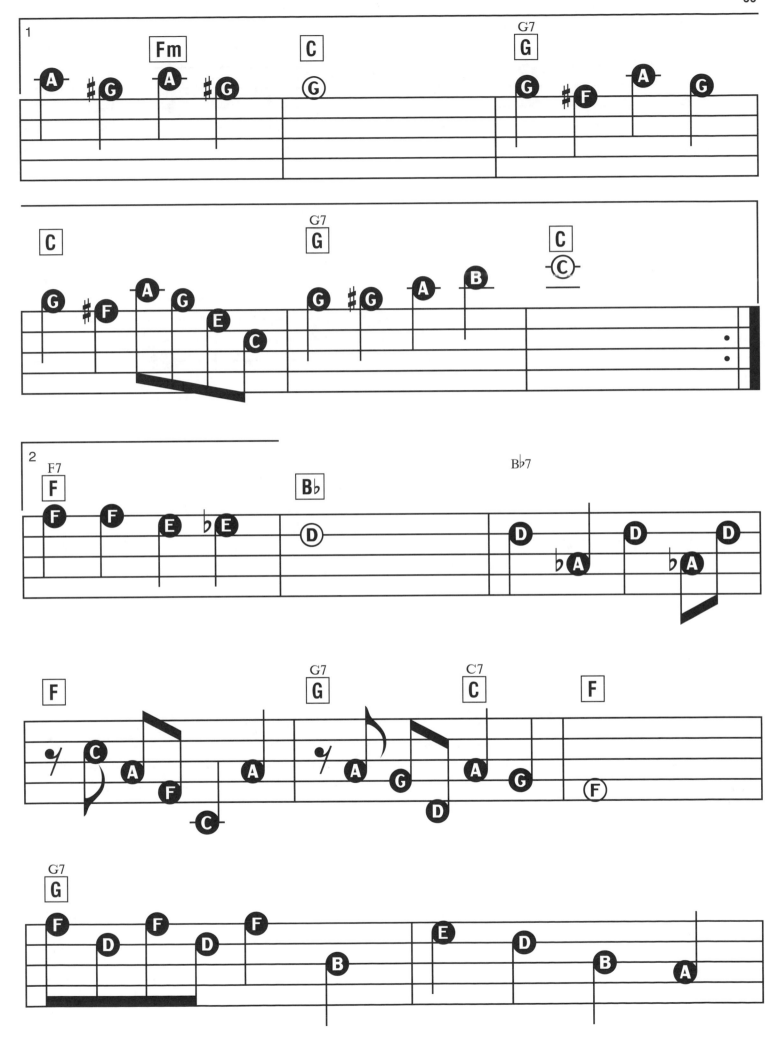

D.C. al Coda
(Return to beginning
Play to ⊕ and
Skip to Coda)

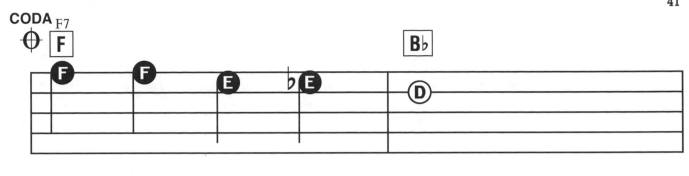

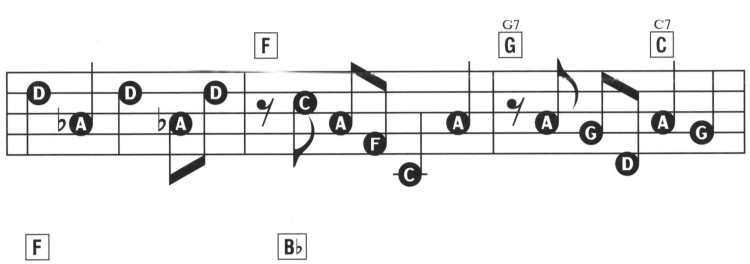

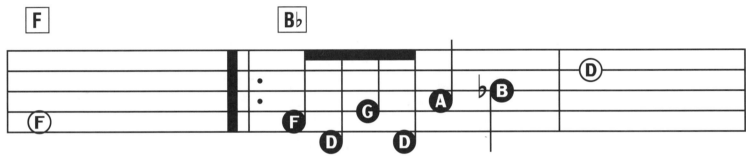

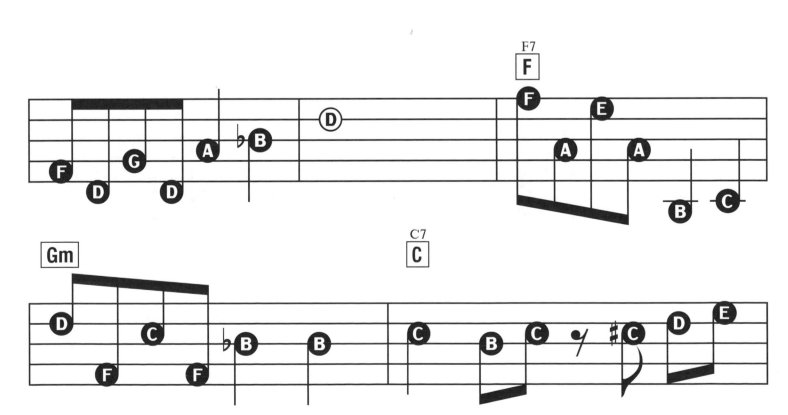

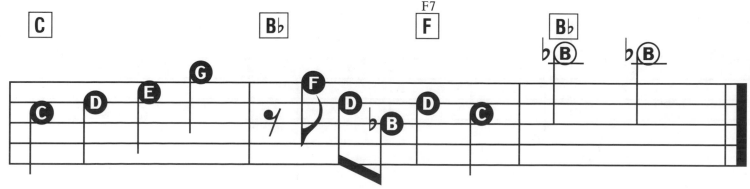

# Rag Time Chimes

Registration 8
Rhythm: Fox Trot

By Percy Wenrich

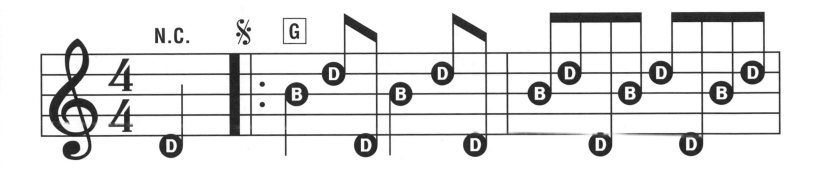

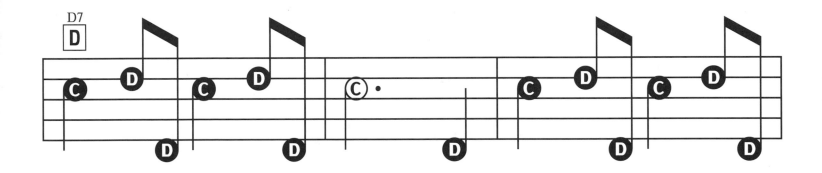

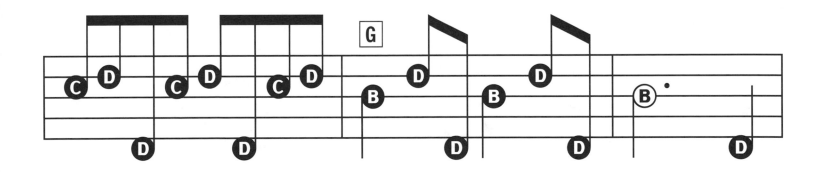

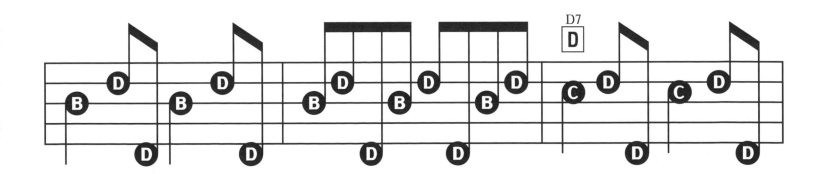

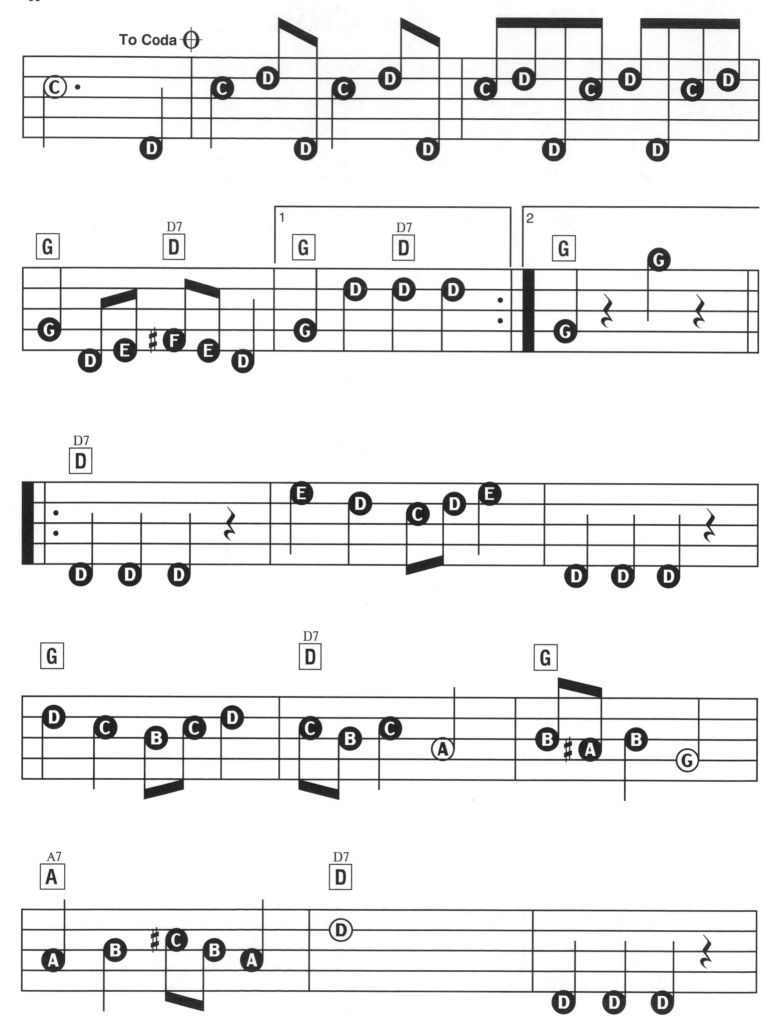

# Sensation Rag

Registration 8
Rhythm: Fox Trot

By Joseph F. Lamb

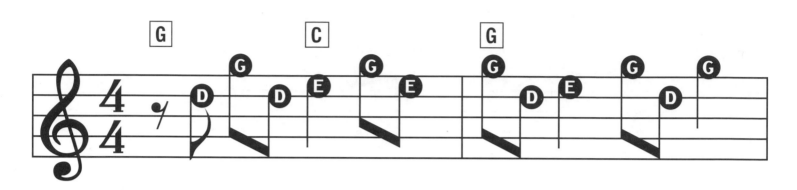

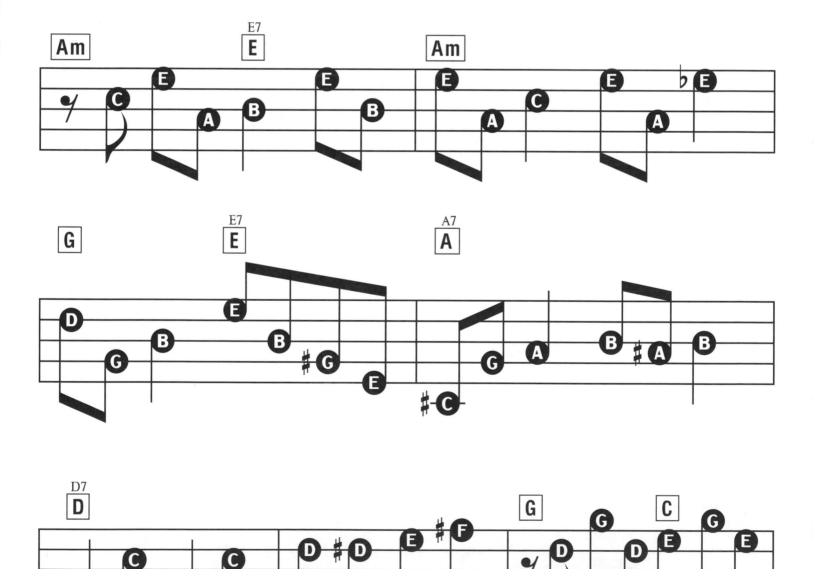

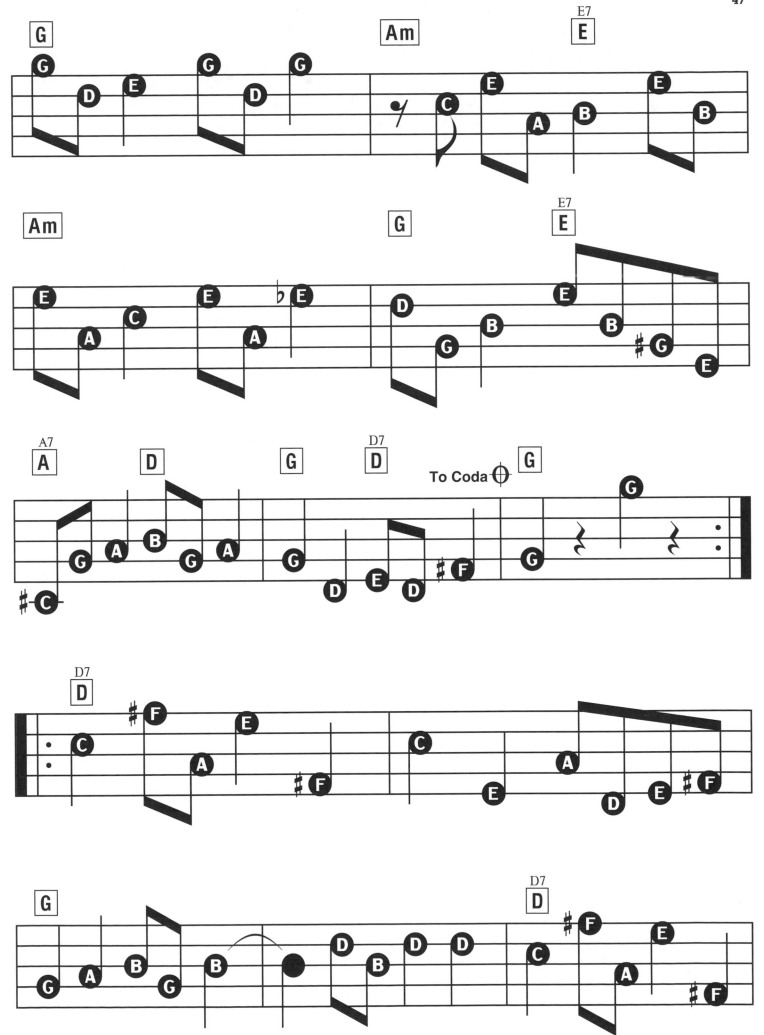

48

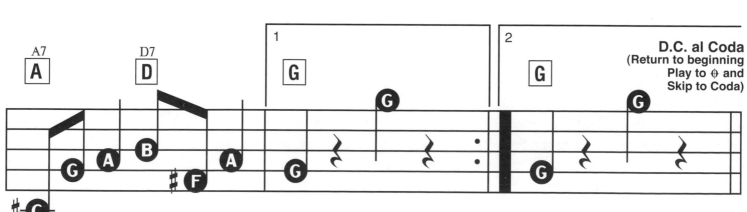

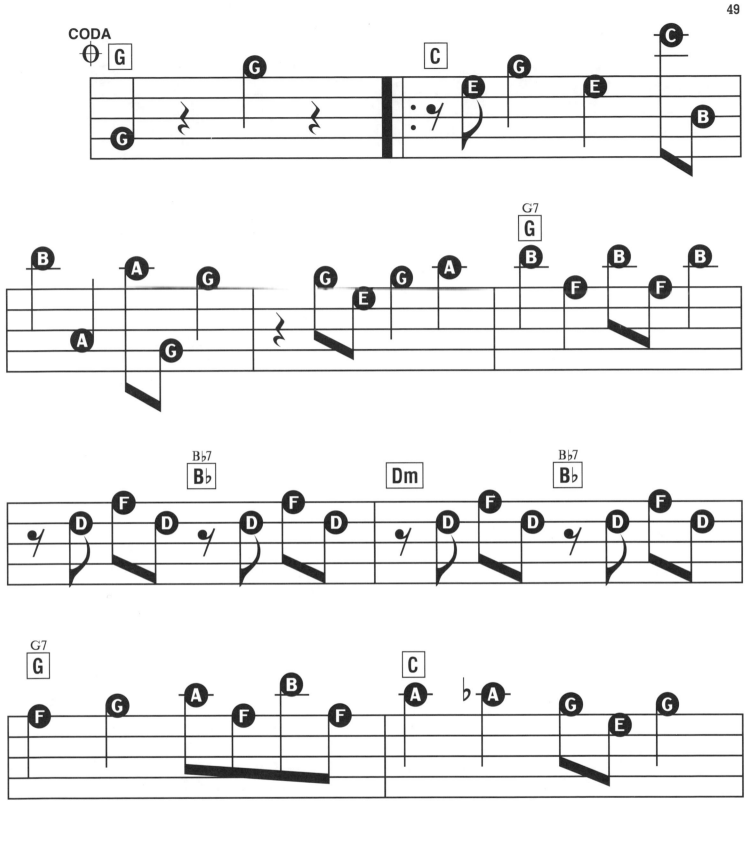

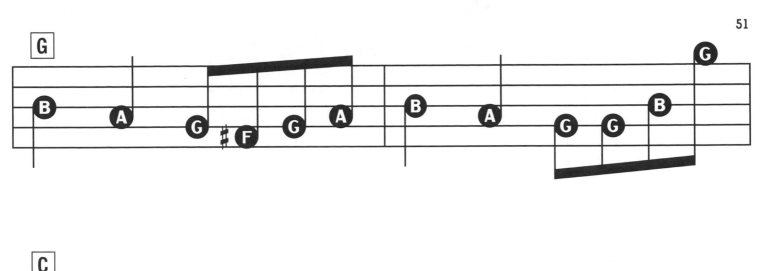

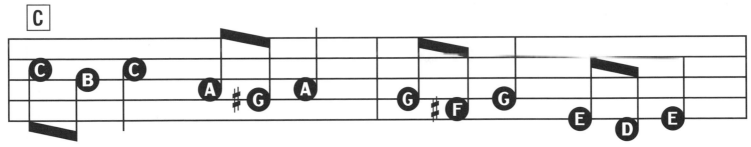

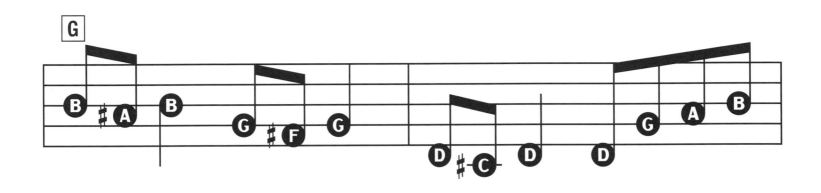

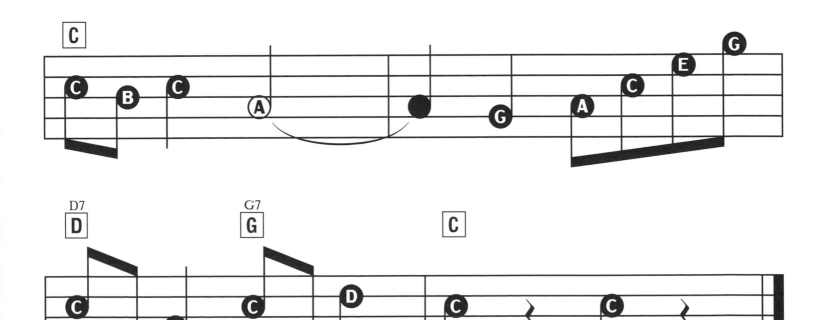

# Something Doing

Registration 8
Rhythm: Fox Trot

By Scott Joplin
and Scott Hayden

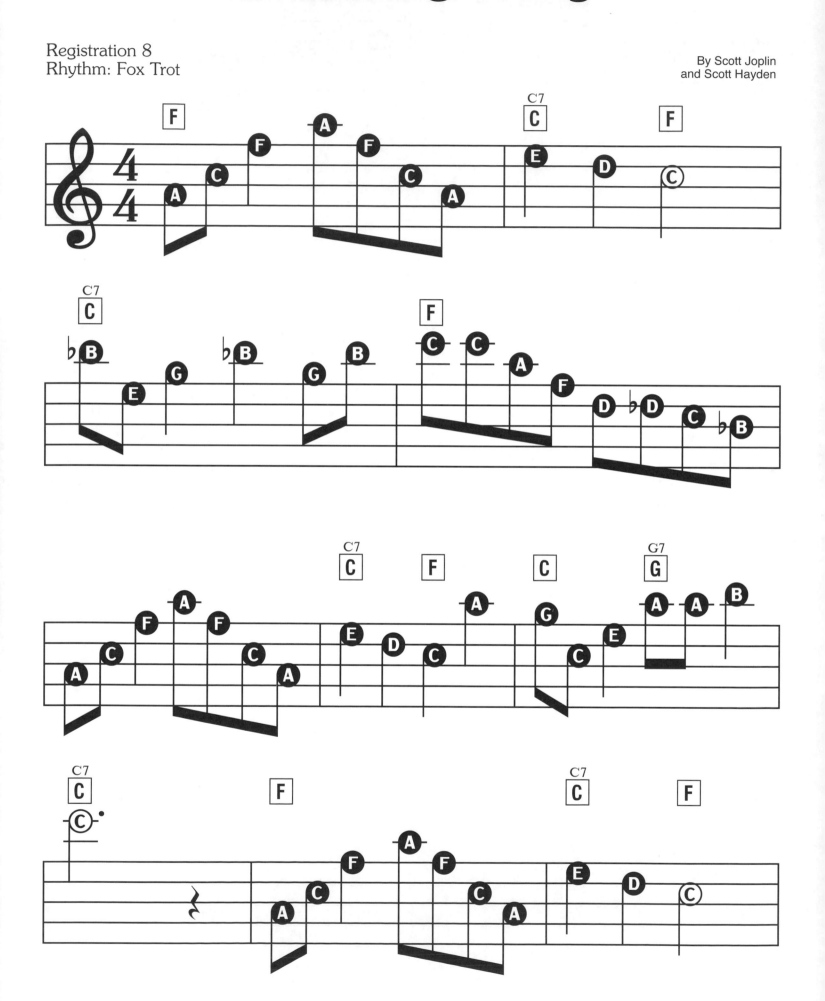

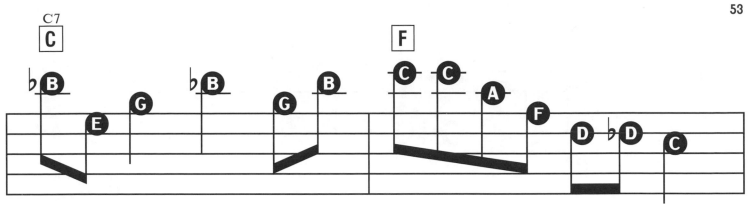

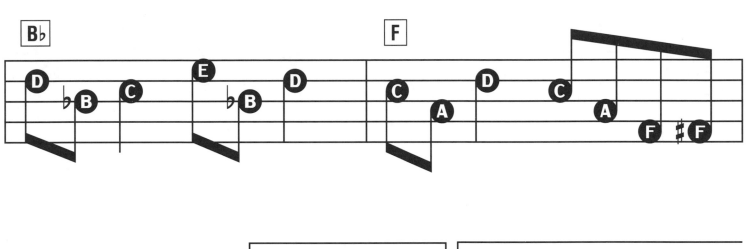

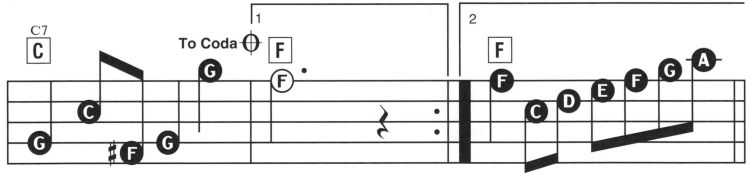

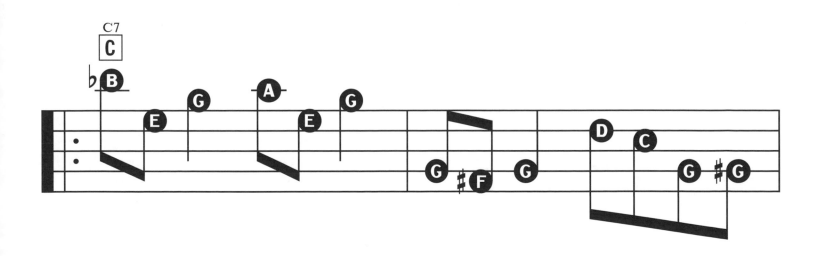

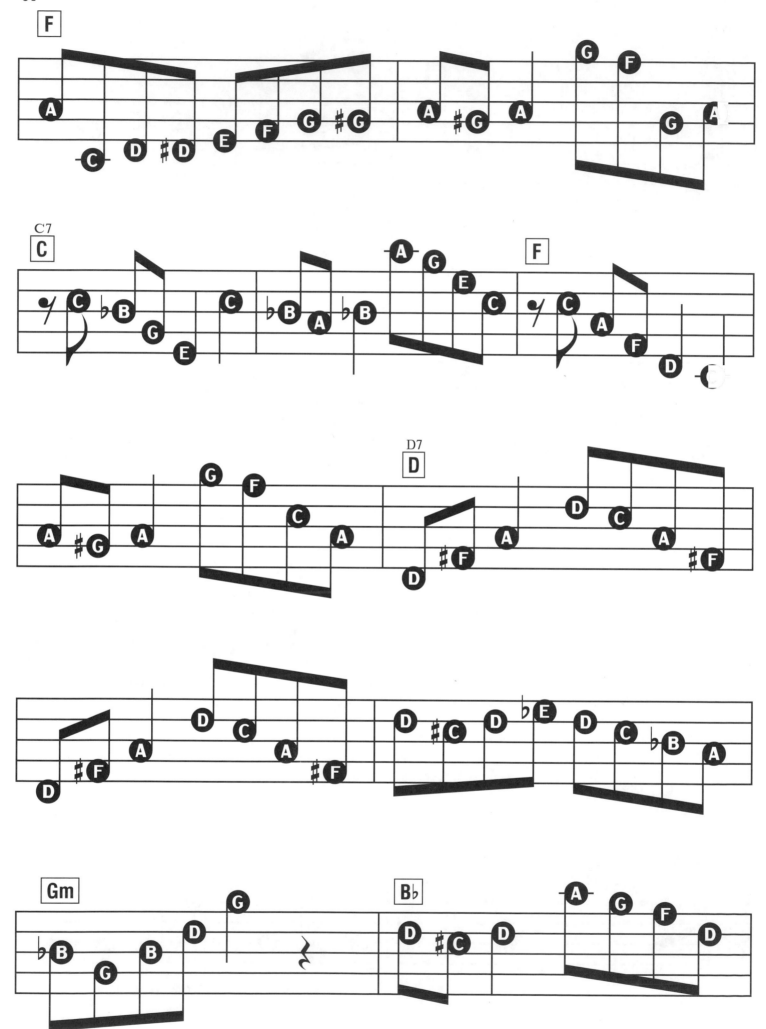

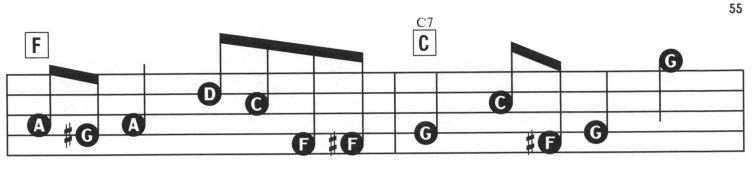

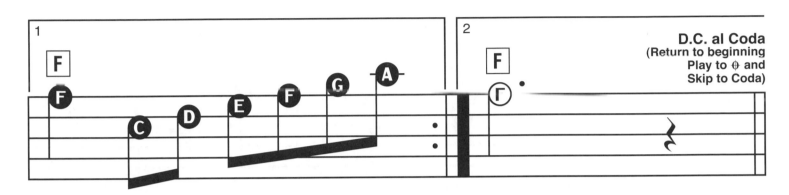

**D.C. al Coda**
(Return to beginning
Play to ⊕ and
Skip to Coda)

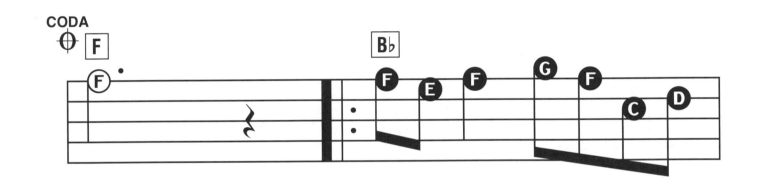

**CODA**

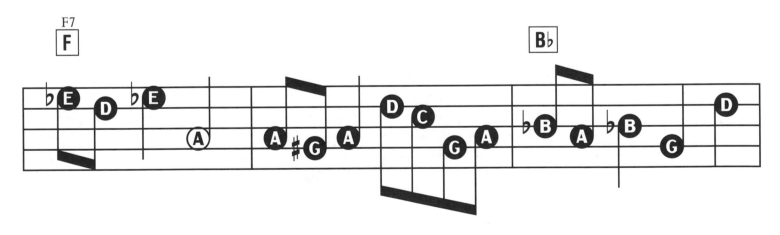

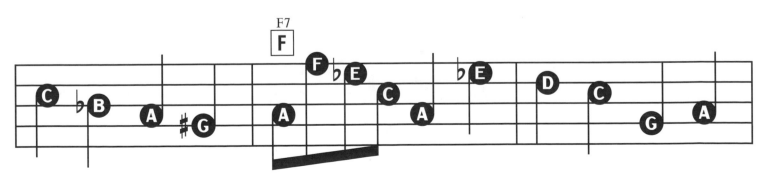

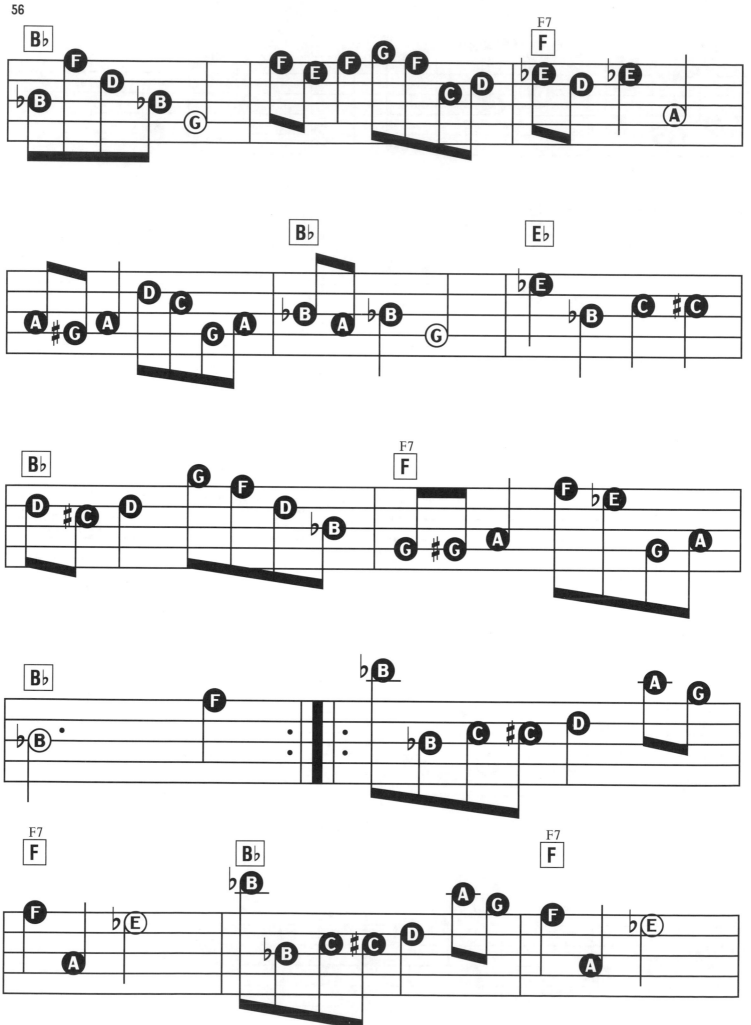

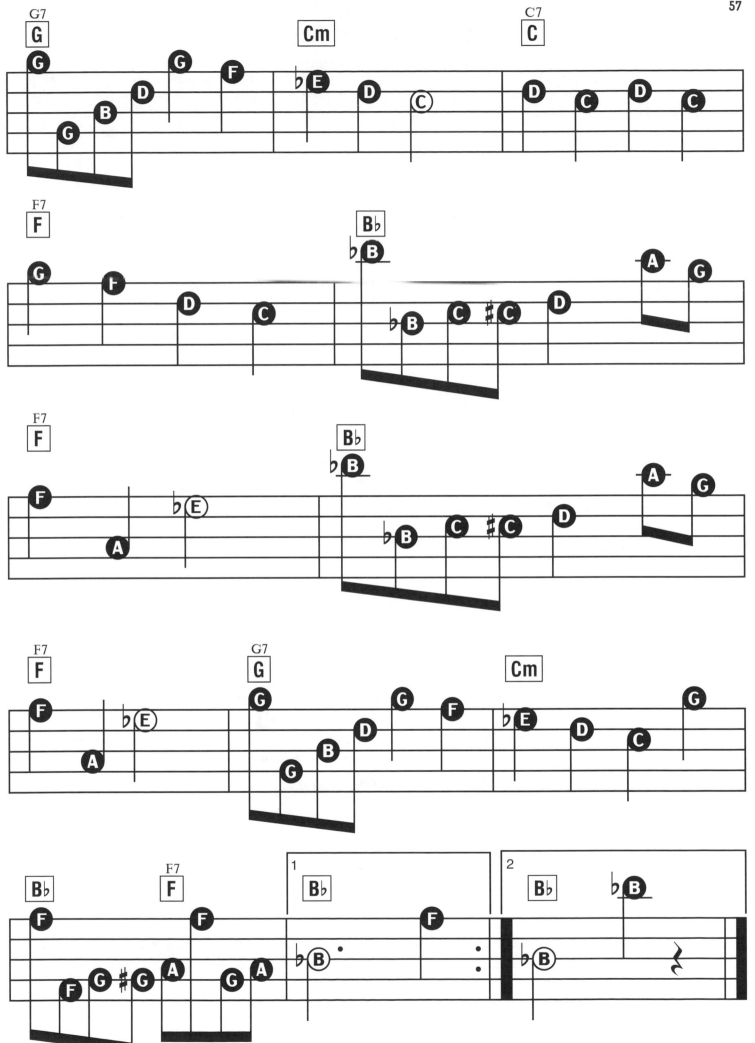

# Tiger Rag

Registration 8
Rhythm: Fox Trot

Attributed to D.J. LaRocca

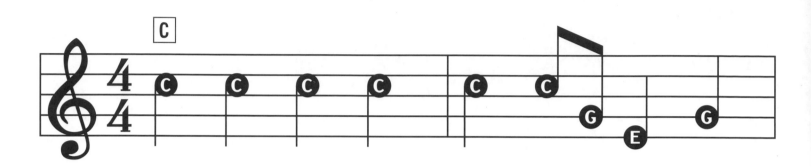

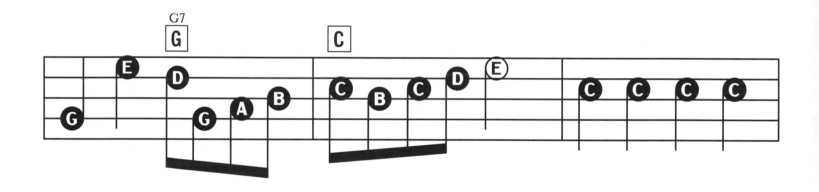

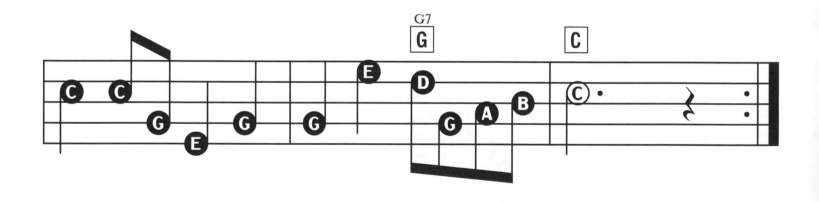

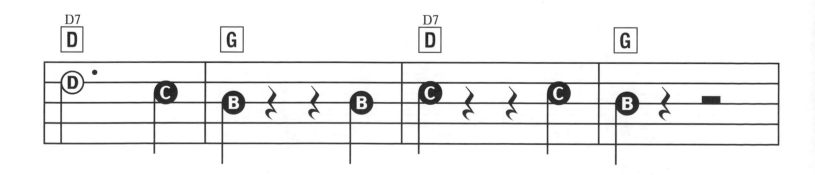

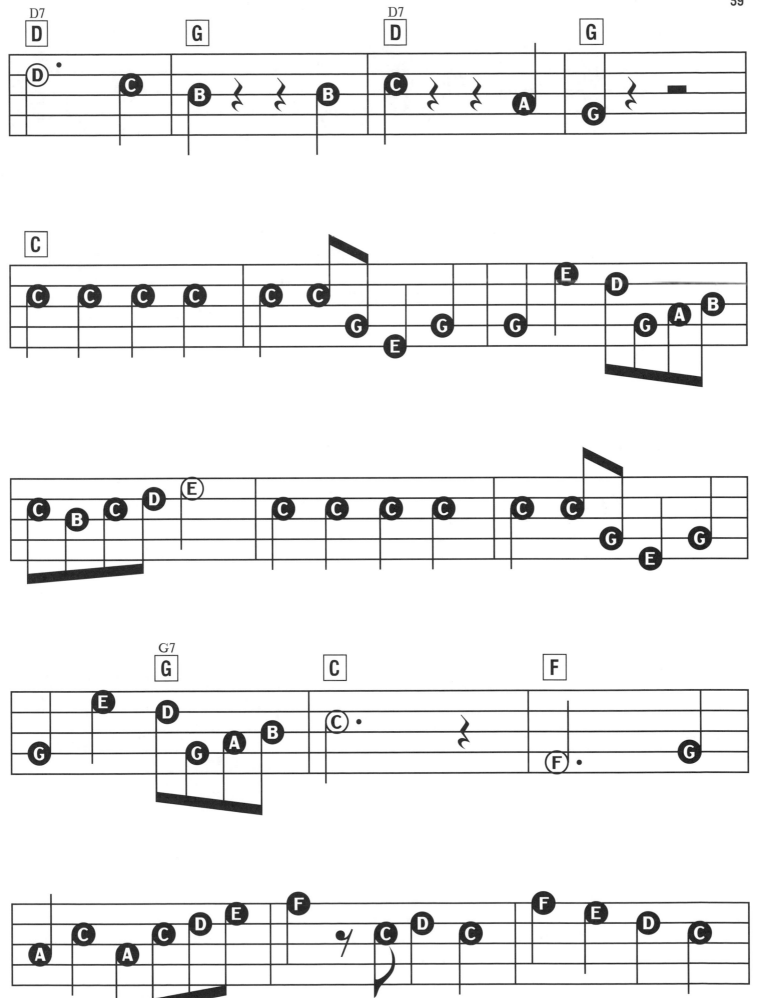

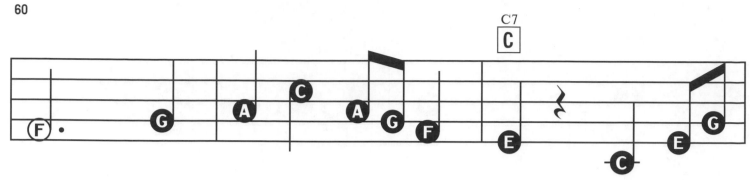

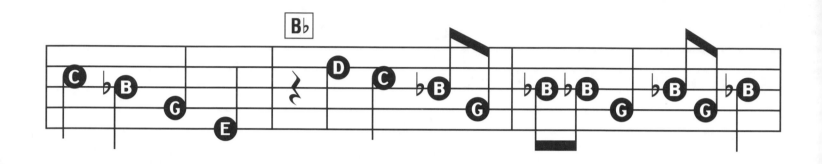

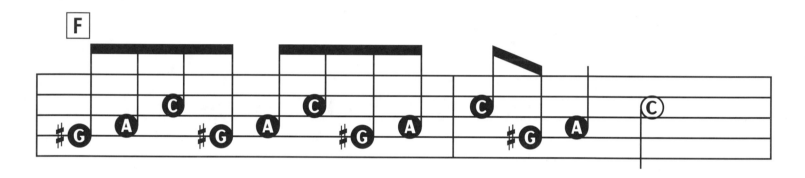

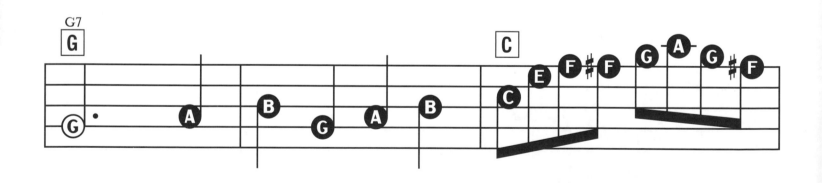

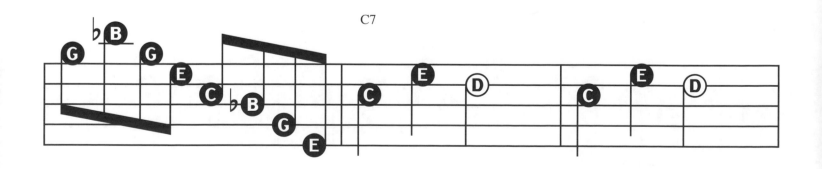

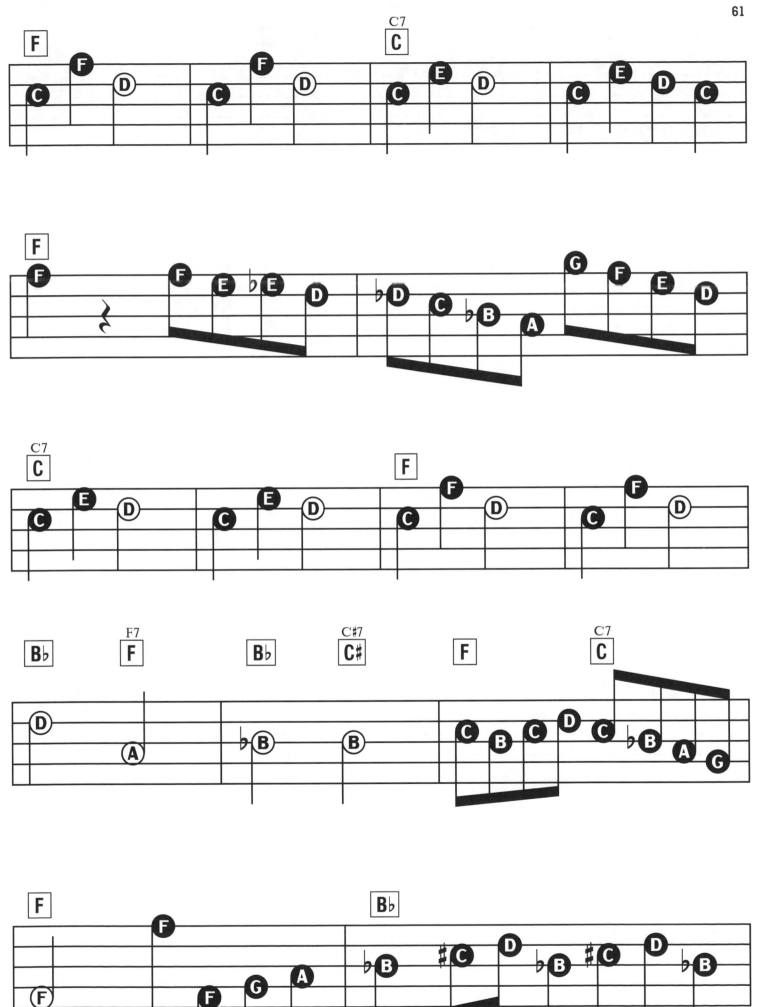

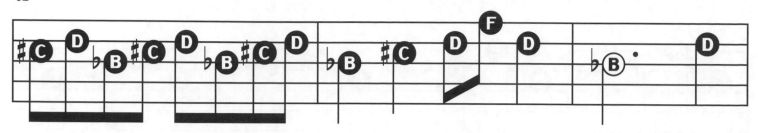

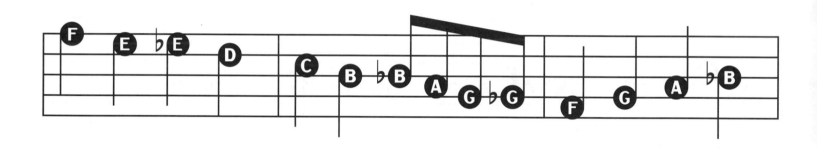

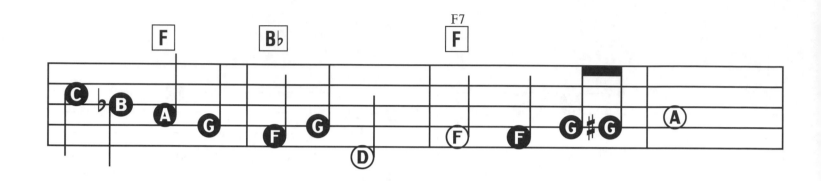

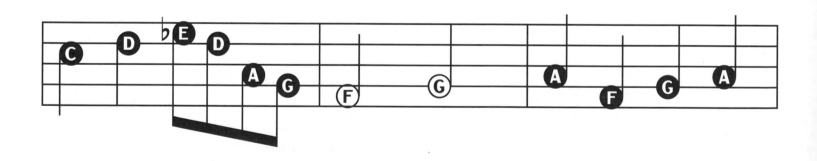

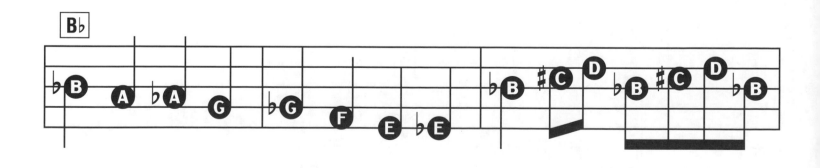

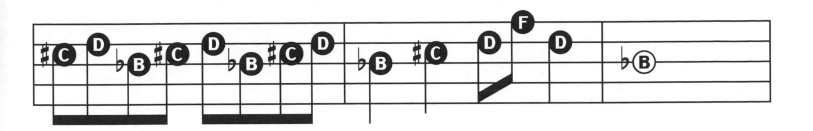

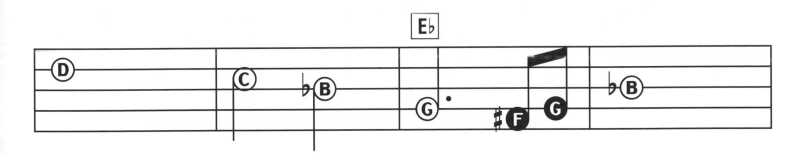

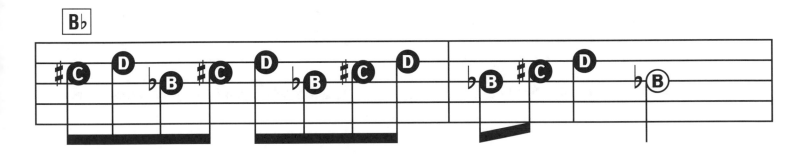

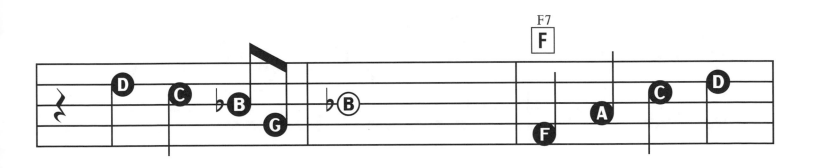

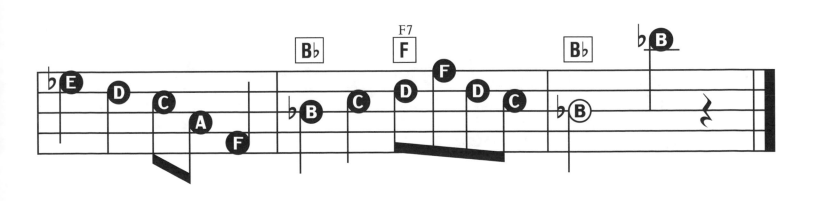

# Twelfth Street Rag

Registration 5
Rhythm: Shuffle or Swing

By Euday L. Bowman

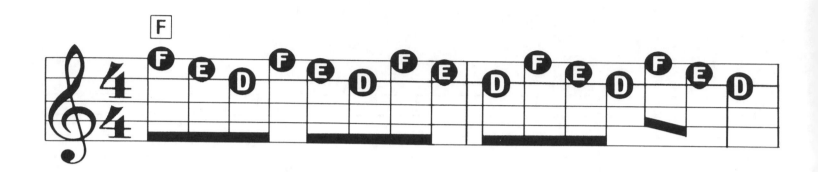

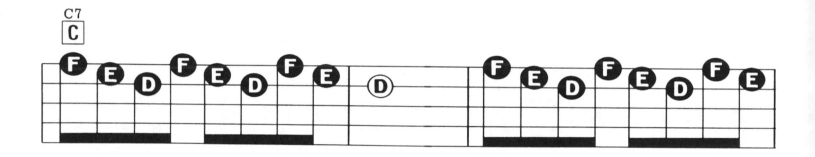

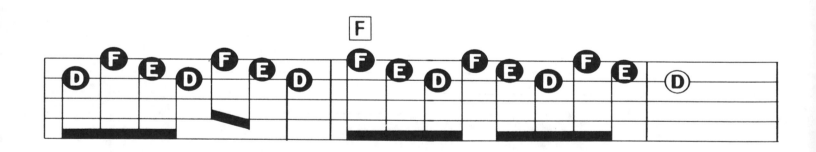

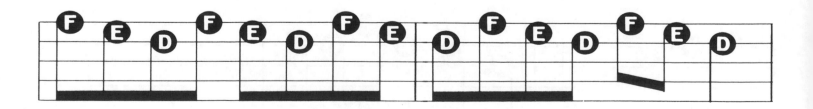

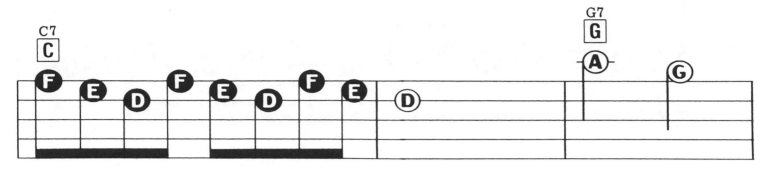

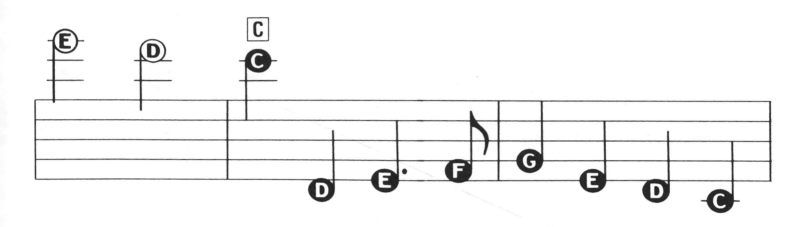

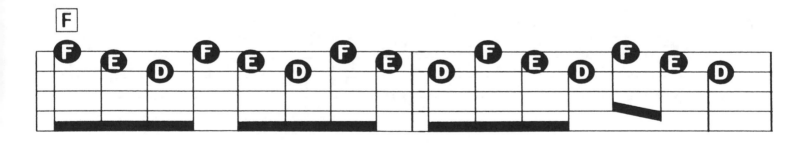

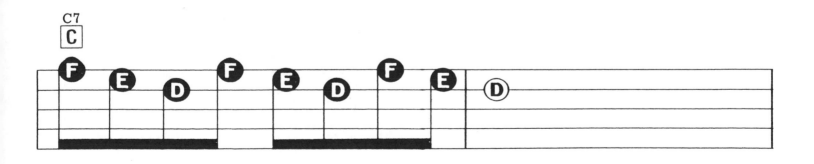

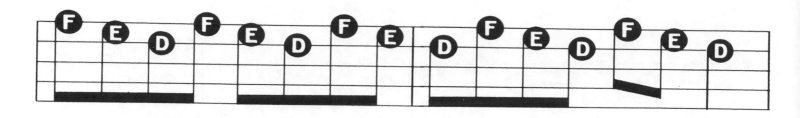

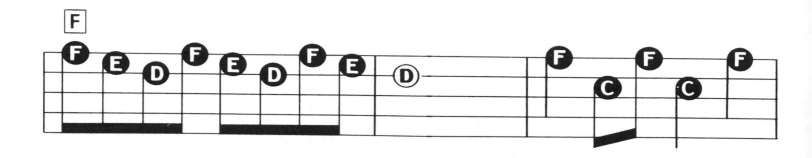

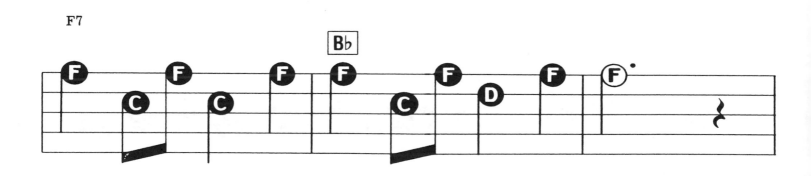

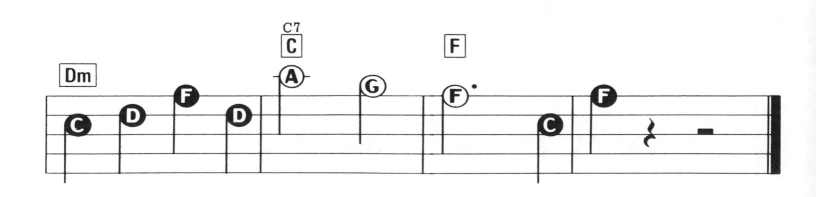

# Weeping Willow

Registration 8
Rhythm: Fox Trot

By Scott Joplin

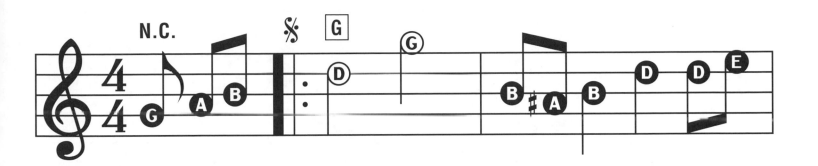

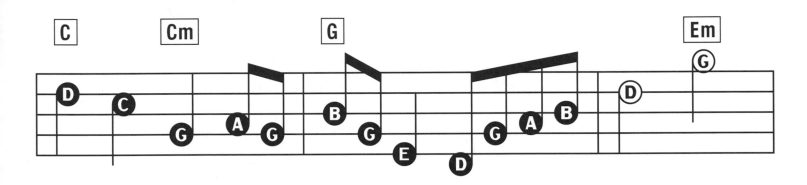

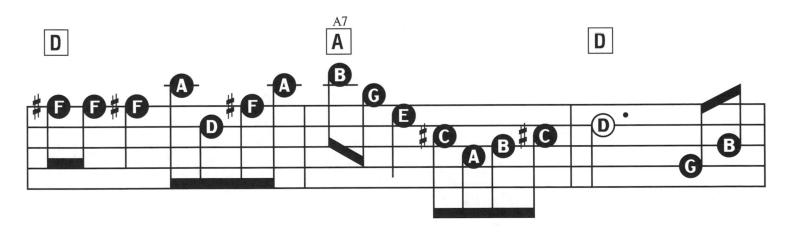

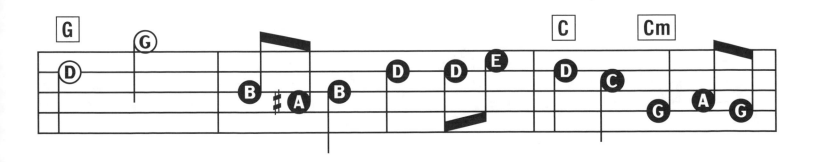

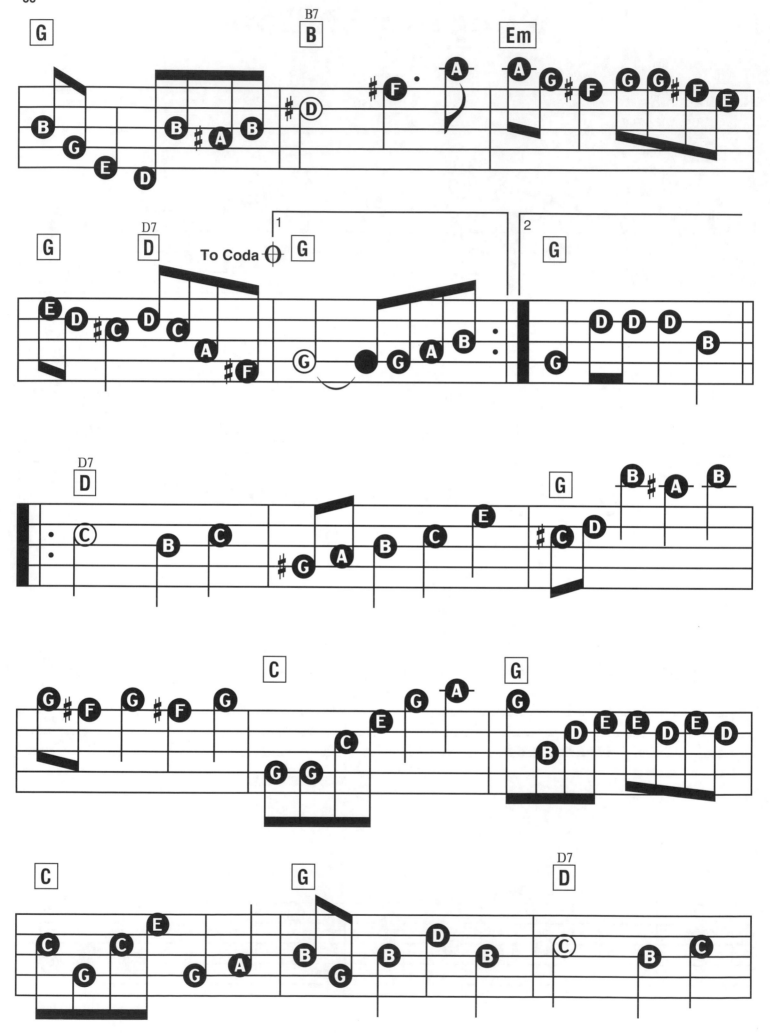

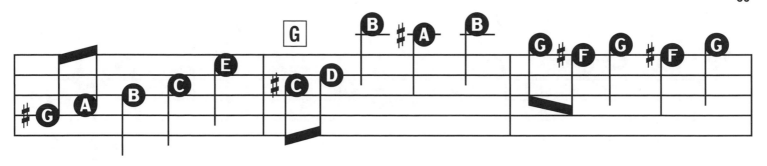

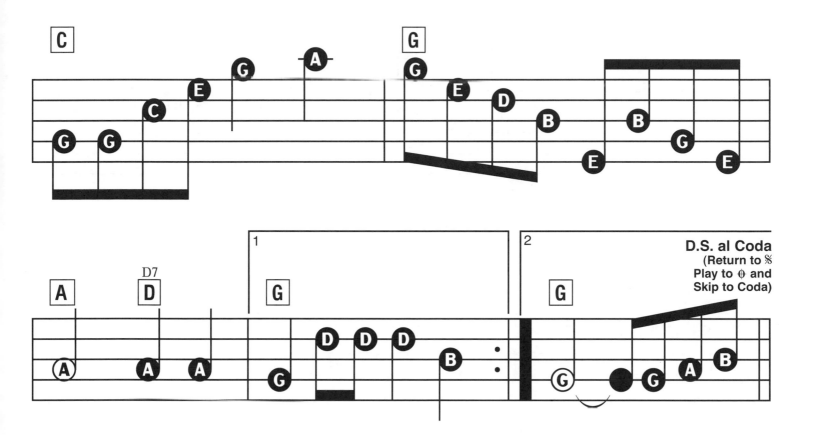

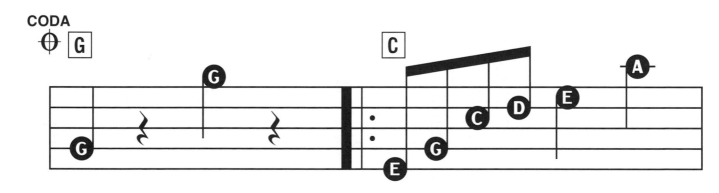

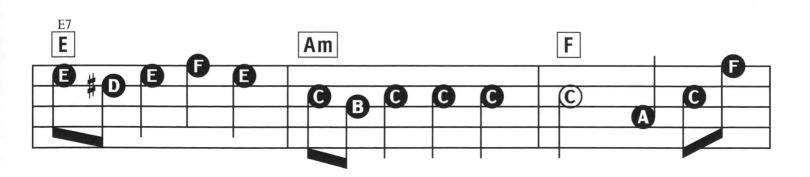

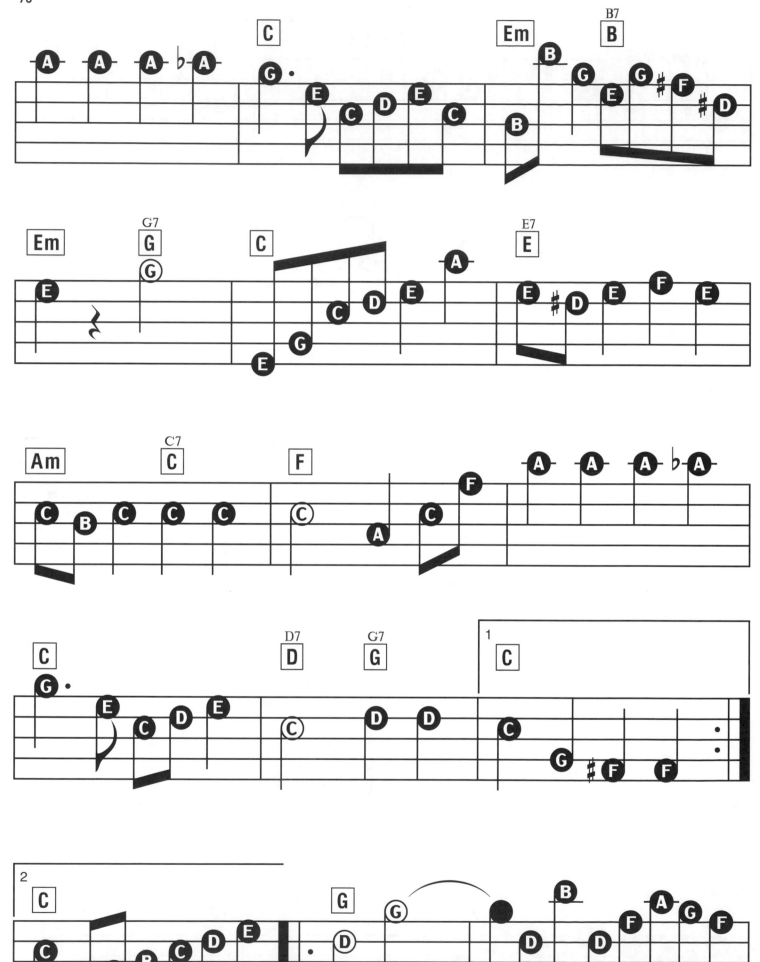

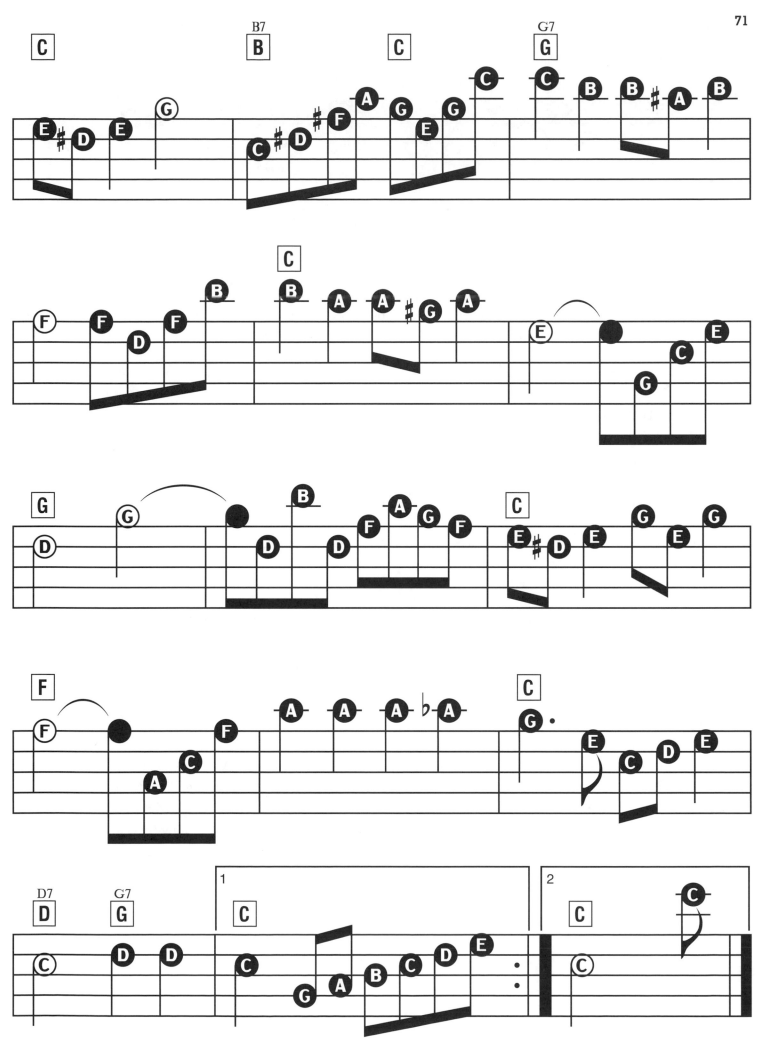

# Registration Guide

• Match the Registration number on the song to the corresponding numbered category below. Select and activate an instrumental sound available on your instrument.

• Choose an automatic rhythm appropriate to the mood and style of the song. (Consult your Owner's Guide for proper operation of automatic rhythm features.)

• Adjust the tempo and volume controls to comfortable settings.

## Registration

| 1 | Mellow | Flutes, Clarinet, Oboe, Flugel Horn, Trombone, French Horn, Organ Flutes |
|---|---|---|
| 2 | Ensemble | Brass Section, Sax Section, Wind Ensemble, Full Organ, Theater Organ |
| 3 | Strings | Violin, Viola, Cello, Fiddle, String Ensemble, Pizzicato, Organ Strings |
| 4 | Guitars | Acoustic/Electric Guitars, Banjo, Mandolin, Dulcimer, Ukulele, Hawaiian Guitar |
| 5 | Mallets | Vibraphone, Marimba, Xylophone, Steel Drums, Bells, Celesta, Chimes |
| 6 | Liturgical | Pipe Organ, Hand Bells, Vocal Ensemble, Choir, Organ Flutes |
| 7 | Bright | Saxophones, Trumpet, Mute Trumpet, Synth Leads, Jazz/Gospel Organs |
| 8 | Piano | Piano, Electric Piano, Honky Tonk Piano, Harpsichord, Clavi |
| 9 | Novelty | Melodic Percussion, Wah Trumpet, Synth, Whistle, Kazoo, Perc. Organ |
| 10 | Bellows | Accordion, French Accordion, Mussette, Harmonica, Pump Organ, Bagpipes |